SILVER ANNIVERSARY EDITION

25 TH

GRAND NATIONAL

ROADSTER SHOW

"Oakland" - The Granddaddy of the AUTO SHOWS

Coliseum Feb. 16-25, 1973

Home Of The Nine-Foot Trophy

SOUVENIR PROGRAM .75

The Oakland Roadster Show

Andy Southard Jr. & Dain Gingerelli

MBI Publishing Company

This book is dedicated to: Al and Mary Slonaker.
Their dream and vision became the hot rod and custom car world's reality.

Chances are there never would have been a Grand National Roadster Show had it not been for the Bay Area's Al and Mary Slonaker. Pictured here during the 1960s, the Slonakers had the foresight to conceive of and promote a car show dedicated specifically for hot rods and customs. Indeed, a promotional fluke that included hot rods during their 1949 general interest car show spawned the idea in the first place for the inaugural National Roadster Show in 1950. And the success of that 1950 show set the foundation for a colorful history that stretches throughout the second half of the 20th century and into the next millennium.

First published in 1998 by MBI Publishing Company, 729 Prospect Avenue, PO Box 1, Osceola, WI 54020-0001 USA

Library of Congress Cataloging-in-Publication Data
    Southard, Andy, Jr., and Gingerelli, Dain.
    The Oakland Roadster Show: 50 years of hot rods and customs/Andy Southard, Jr. & Dain Gingerelli
        p. cm.
    Includes index.
    ISBN 0-7603-0608-7 (pbk.: alk. paper)
    1. Grand National Roadster Show (Oakland)—History. 2. Hot rods—California—Oakland —Exhibitions—History. I. Southard, Andy. II. Title.
TL7.U620234   1998
629.228'6'07479466—dc21   98-42470

On the front cover: The "America's Most Beautiful Roadster" award at the 1995 show went to Fred Warren, with his *Smoothster*, a 1937 Ford painted pearl yellow. The car was based on a Larry Erickson design, and eventually went to Boyd Coddington who finished construction for Warren. The car had Corvette front and rear suspension with disc brakes, 1992 Corvette LT1 engine, and 700R4 transmission. The Carson-style one-piece top is covered with dark tan canvas material.

On the frontispiece: This priceless program, commemorating the 25th Silver Anniversary Edition of the Grand National Roadster Show, belongs to Bruce Heather. The silver anniversary program was signed by many of Oakland's legendary car builders. Note the program's 75-cent price.

Look closely at the historical autographs, fourteen in all. They are from left to right: Bill Cushenbery, Tommy The Greek, Rod Powell, Joe Ortiz Customs, George Barris, Gene Winfield, Bill Gaylord-Gaylord Top and Interiors, Norm Grabowski, Gordon Vann-Auto Body, Joe Bailon-Bailon Customs, Darryl Starbird-Star Custom Shop, Joe Wilhelm, Dean Jeffries-The Great Days, Alexander Brothers-Larry & Mike "A" Bros. Truly a one-of-a-kind collectible.

On the title page: The Grand National Roadster Show was first held at the Oakland Exposition Building, located on Fallon Street, in 1950. In 1968 the show moved to the newly constructed Oakland Coliseum. It wasn't until 1997 that the show relocated again, this time to the Coliseum's parking lot! The temporary move was due to rennovation for the Coliseum complex; that show was held in two huge tents. The following year a schedule conflict forced the Oakland Roadster Show to move out of town for the first time in its 49-year history. And so the 1998 show was held at the Concourse Exhibition Center in San Francisco. The 50th Anniversary Show, scheduled for February 10-15, 1999, will be at the Cow Palace in South San Francisco. This photograph reveals a bevy of beautiful roadsters at the 1979 show. The red 1932 Ford was owned by Brian Burnett, that year's "America's Most Beautiful Roadster."

On the back cover: Oakland Roadster Show, 1956: This '32 Ford roadster, owned by Harry Love Jr. of Redwood City, California, is a fine example of an early hot rod. The highboy has all the hardware of a traditional hot rod, including a chopped windshield, dropped-and-filled front axle, chromed backing plates, and custom headlight bar. The interior was completed with red and white Naugahyde and Stewart Warner gauges. Beneath the hood sat a '48 Mercury flathead with Edelbrock high-compression heads and three carburetors. Cars such as this helped make the Oakland Roadster Show America's premier hot rod and custom car show from the very beginning.

On the back cover, inset: The Grand National Roadster Show is known for its customs, too. Shown here is an outstanding custom owned by Frank Livingston of San Leandro, California. The *Crown Jewel* looks as though it were built back in the 1950s, but it is actually a new custom. It's a '49 Chevy fastback set on a '79 Oldsmobile chassis. Mix in a Chevy 350 V-8 for power, and you've got the basis of a cool ride. Livingston debuted The *Crown Jewel* at the 49th Grand National Roadster Show in January, 1998.

Designed by Todd Sauers

Printed in Hong Kong through World Print, Ltd.

Contents

Acknowledgments

Generally, the creation of a hot rod or custom car does not happen overnight. Neither does it result from the hard work of a single person. Instead, most rods and customs are nurtured to life by a group of craftsmen and builders who share their ideas, and call upon one another to provide specific skills so that the end product is truly a unique, one-of-a-kind car.

Fittingly, the genesis and growth of this book closely parallels the evolutionary process of a typical hot rod or custom car that would be built to compete at the Grand National Roadster Show itself. This book is not the single effort of one, or even two, authors. Instead, *The Oakland Roadster Show: 50 Years of Hot Rods & Customs* is the culmination of 50 years hard work by many of the leading hot rod and custom car builders in the country. But even those artisans represent only a fraction of the cast of characters, for behind the scenes countless other people continue to play a major role in the annual production that we call the Grand National Roadster Show. It begins with the show's promoter, and trickles down to the show's general manager and car show judges and trophy girls, and the people working the aisles and vendor displays, and the ticket takers and parking lot attendants and floor sweepers.

There's also another group of unsung heroes that have become an integral part of making the Grand National Roadster Show the premier custom car event in the country. This group consists of the automotive journalists who, every year, publish their Oakland Roadster Show reports in the leading hot rod and custom car magazines. Year in and year out they ply the show floor, photographing the glamorous show cars, interviewing the builders and owners, and generally gathering information for their stories. The fruits of their labor can be found within the magazine pages, preserving forever the events and winners of each and every Grand National Roadster Show that has taken place since 1950.

It's those people, among many others, who the authors wish to acknowledge. In particular, we thank Oakland Roadster Show promoters Mary Slonaker, Harold "Baggy" Bagdasarian, and Don Tognotti; show general manager Rick Perry; and the following automotive journalists: Griff Borgeson (*Hot Rod Magazine*), LeRoi "Tex" Smith (*HRM*), Spence Murray (*Rod & Custom*), Bill Neumann, (*R&C*), Pat Ganahl (*R&C*), Geoff Carter (*Street Rodder Magazine*), Steve Coonan (*SRM*), Eric Geisert (*SRM*), Jerry Weesner (*SRM*), Dick Mendonca (*Rod Action Magazine*), Thom Taylor (*American Rodder Magazine*), Mike Bishop (*ARM*), and Mike Griffin (*ARM*).

A small army of Oakland Roadster Show enthusiasts also played a role in making this book a reality. Among them are: Bruce Heather whose collection of Oakland memorabilia and show programs from 1950 through 1973 proved invaluable to our research, and Dave Cunningham and Frank Faraone for their archive photos from the early years of Oakland.

Furthermore, the authors wish to thank the following people for their unselfish contributions and use of their archive photos, or for relating their personal experiences at Oakland during the show's 50-year past. Thanks to: Bob and Rosemary Accosta; Joe Bailon; George Barris; Don Bell; Pete Biro; Andy and Sue Brizio; Roy Brizio; Vince Burgos; Chic Cannon; Tom Cutino; Ken Fuhrman; Blackie Gejeian; Don Graham; Mike Homen; John LaBelle; Bud Millard; Rudy Perez; Rod Powell; Don Reid; Nick Reynal; Ed "Big Daddy" Roth; Greg Sharp; Clyde Smith; and Don Varner. Your insight and cooperation is beyond description. Thanks also to Keith Mathiowetz of MBI Publishing Company for enduring our panicking telephone calls, and for keeping the faith that this concise history of Oakland was worth the effort.

Finally, the authors wish to thank our wives who, through their unyielding support, helped us meet the abbreviated deadline imposed for this book. Thanks to Patty Southard and Donna Gingerelli. Your love and support made it all bearable.

—*Andy Southard Jr., Salinas, California.*
—*Dain Gingerelli, Mission Viejo, California.*

Introduction

The Makings of a Grand Event

From tiny acorns mighty oaks grow, so goes the saying. But for members of the hot rod and custom car community, that single-sentence parable equally could state: from a tiny car show mighty Oakland grew. Oakland for car people, of course, means only one thing—the Grand National Roadster Show, held annually in Oakland, California, a blue-collar community nestled along the rolling hills on the east side of cold and windy San Francisco Bay.

The Grand National Roadster Show came to be known simply as Oakland for several reasons, among them that the event's official and rather lengthy title constantly proved to be a mouthful of words for spectators and participants to say and was a pageful of print for writers to include in their annual show reports. The logical substitute became, simply, "Oakland," in reference to the city where the show takes place every year on or before President's Day weekend. So Oakland it is, and to this day that single-word moniker works for practically everybody associated with the event. Consequently, when you mention Oakland to a car nut, it's the same—only quicker and easier—as saying Grand National Roadster Show.

The Grand National Roadster Show has another nickname: it's often referred to as the "Granddaddy" of all hot rod and custom car shows, for this is the oldest event of its kind in the world, marking its 50th anniversary February 10–15, 1999. The first Grand National Roadster Show was held in 1950, and no other custom car show of this magnitude has been around longer. In short, Oakland is to hot rod car show enthusiasts what the Indy 500 is to race fans or what Pebble Beach is to members of the classic car fraternity.

But if you dig deep into the past you'll discover that Oakland's roots reach even beyond 1950, back to early 1949, to be precise. That's when an enterprising young couple, Al and Mary Slonaker, promoted Oakland's first-ever hot rod show in the old Exposition Building on the corner of 10th and Fallon Streets. There was no "Grand" or

"National" in that show's title. In fact, the show's name didn't even make reference to hot rods, or roadsters for that matter. Simply, the weekend event was an international-type car show, an event that fed on America's rekindled hunger for the automobile. America's car cravings were especially pronounced by 1949 because it had been less than four years since World War II had ended, so the nation's peacetime auto industry had yet to regain full speed. New cars remained somewhat of a novelty in January of 1949.

Yet, while people like the Slonakers were enraptured with fancy new cars from Europe and Detroit, a small core of enthusiasts in America had been marching to the beat of their own drum. Those enthusiasts were hot rodders, and when a dedicated group in the Bay Area got word of the Slonakers' event, they made an end run to be included in the show.

Recalls Mary Slonaker today: "The first show (1949) was actually an international auto show. We didn't invite the hot rods because, quite frankly, Al and I didn't even know what hot rods were. We'd never seen one before. We were more into foreign cars, rallies, things like that."

But shortly before that first show in 1949 began, the Slonakers got their first taste of what these modified cars were all about when a small group of Bay Area hot rodders asked if they could display their cars in the Exposition Building alongside the foreign cars. The Slonakers agreed, or, as Mary recalls years later, "We gave them a little corner (of the building)." And that was the extent of promotion for the home-built mongrels that shared the show floor with what amounted to factory-bred pedigreed sports cars.

There were no grand displays adorned with flashing lights, mirrors, or angel hair, for that matter, to enhance the hot rods' beauty. Those kinds of props would come later. Instead, the cars were parked impassively in the old armory building so that spectators could see up close what a hot rod was all about.

According to Mary, only about 10 hot rods were displayed in the Exposition Building for that first show. That handful of hot rods shared the spotlight with about 70 or 80 "foreign cars," as Mary puts it. Interestingly, by the end of the weekend, it was clear that the spectators showed more interest in the hodgepodge grouping of hot rods than they did for the new sports and imported cars that highlighted the marquee.

Fortunately for hot rodding, Al Slonaker was a shrewd promoter and businessman, and he knew a winner when he saw one. It was an asset that he acquired while working in the publicity department of the World's Fair (which had been held in San Francisco shortly before the outbreak of World War II), giving him insight into what people did and didn't like. When Al Slonaker noticed the attention that the hot rods commanded at his international auto show—his first endeavor of this sort—he pulled his wife and business partner to the side and said to her, "Next year we're going to do things differently."

Doing things "differently" meant one thing in particular—their auto show would feature hot rods only. No foreign cars, no new cars, only hot rods. As a result, the microcosmic world of hot rodding added two new members to its ranks. Those two newcomers were Al and Mary Slonaker, and as history would prove, their work in promoting an event that eventually was to become known as the Grand National Roadster Show would become a key factor in unifying hot rodding into the huge, and rather autonomous, industry that it has become today.

The next 11 months leading to 1950 were spent scouting the Bay Area's rank and file hot rodders to see how they felt about an all-hot-rod show for the following January. The Slonakers were met with an enthusiastic "yes!" from everybody that they talked to about the next year's show.

Despite Oakland's longevity for being the oldest custom car show on the calendar today, it was not the first event of this sort. Actually, before the Slonakers opened shop at the Oakland Exposition Building for their 1950 show, there had been several other hot rod shows promoted in California—by 1948 considered the hotbed of hot rodding.

Among the first of these pre-Oakland shows was a small hot rod display promoted by Gene Winfield, a young, wide-eyed kid from the Central Valley who loved cars, especially customs and racers. Winfield's first event was held in 1949 at a Ford dealership in his hometown of Modesto, California. Winfield went on to become one of the country's most acclaimed custom car builders—to this day he is responsible for some beautiful customs and hot rods— while his show remained a part of the West Coast custom car show scene until 1969.

Perhaps the first hot rod show of magnitude was the Southern California Timing Association's (SCTA) famed two-day rodders' regalia at the Armory Building in Los Angeles, California, held in January 1948. That show's purpose was twofold. Obviously, the SCTA members wanted to showcase their fine hot rods to the public, and this event gave them that opportunity. In so doing, they hoped to achieve another goal, and that was to make the public aware that hot rodders weren't just a bunch of young, wild-eyed hooligans who practiced blatant disregard for the law. By the end of the show, the SCTA members' message was clear: hot rodders were people, too.

The Armory show in Los Angeles marked another hot rod milestone, the official debut of *Hot Rod* magazine. But just as Oakland wasn't the first custom car show, *Hot Rod* was not the first magazine dedicated to the sport of hot rodding. However, it was the first periodical to prosper and thrive, making it the touchstone of the sport during the following 50 years. From its inception, *Hot Rod* magazine was published in Los Angeles, and the initial issues focused primarily on local hot rodding news, especially SCTA dry lakes racing. As the publication grew in circulation and size, it gained broader insights for its editorial direction. Within a few years, the magazine regularly featured news and events from around the country.

The forthcoming Oakland hot rod show in 1950 proved to be one of those non-Southern California feature stories. In fact, the announcement of a new trophy that would be awarded to the top winner of the 1950 Oakland hot rod show appeared in the October 1949 issue of *Hot Rod*. The new trophy, featured in *Hot Rod*'s famous "Parts with Appeal" section, stood eight feet tall (it was later advertised as nine feet tall), and the inscription on its base read "America's Most Beautiful Roadster." Actress Barbara Britton posed with the trophy (thus, the "appeal" in "Parts with Appeal"), which gave further credence to hot rods in general, and to the Oakland show in particular. Before the Exposition Building's doors even opened, the Slonaker's hot rod show had meaning, purpose, merit, and most of all, significance.

The Slonakers realized this, too, as did *Hot Rod*'s editors. And so, to promote the trophy, the show was given a new and unique title—National Roadster Show.

Today it might seem strange that the show was called a *roadster* show. Why not *hot rod* or even *custom car* show? Good question, and for that we must look back at postwar hot rodding for a clearer picture of what hot rodding was like during its infancy years.

Foremost, it's safe to say that hot rodding's genesis can be pinpointed to roadster cars rather than to coupes and sedans because hot rodders themselves recognized their open-top cars as *true* candidates for modifications. Roadsters, by general definition, are single-seat, open-top cars that don't have roll-up windows. Among the most popular roadsters for early-day hot rodding were Fords, specifically the Model T, Model A, and the venerable '32 "Deuce," which also happened to be Ford Motor Company's first entry with a V-8 engine. Ford continued making roadsters through 1937, but for the most part the roadster's final five model years weren't as well received by rodders as were the Model T, Model A, and Deuce roadsters.

The roadster movement was especially popular among the dry lakes racing crowd. In fact, until 1949, the SCTA's rules allowed only roadsters, modifieds, and streamliners to compete in the speed trials. Prior to that date, if a hot rod with a hard top showed up at an SCTA meet, it sat on the sidelines, and was ineligible to race for championship points and speed records. Ultimately, though, the SCTA's rules were changed to recognize closed-top cars such as coupes and sedans. (It's important to note that other clubs, including the Russetta Timing Association, allowed closed-top cars from the beginning.)

Roadster elitism found its way onto the street, too, and many of the early-day hot rod clubs contained the word *roadster* in their names. Among those early-day clubs were the Glendale Coupe and Roadster Club, the San Diego Roadster Club, the Pasadena Roadster Club, and, of course, the Oakland Roadster Club.

The Pasadena Roadsters were among the first to promote a bona fide street event, known as the Pasadena Reliability Run, first held in 1948. As the name suggests, the Pasadena Reliability Run was a test to see how road-worthy your hot rod *roadster* really was. The run started at the Rose Bowl in Pasadena, California, then wound its way through the nearby San Gabriel Mountains, culminating about 130 miles away at a predesignated location (or back to the Rose Bowl) that the entries navigated to in their hot rod roadsters.

About this same time quarter-mile drag racing was gaining a foothold in the sport. Early attempts at staging drag races included solo events at Goleta (California) Airport and Mile Square Airport (in what is now Fountain Valley, California). It wasn't until July 3, 1950, that the Orange County Drags—the first continuously run drag strip—opened at Santa Ana (California) Airport. Within the next year, drag races were held in the Northern California town of Salinas, plus in such far away places as Texas, Tennessee, and Colorado.

By 1949 the sport of hot rodding was growing at a rapid rate, which was good news for the Slonakers, who

had reserved the weekend of January 19–22, 1950, for their first official hot rod show. And, with the editorial backing of *Hot Rod* magazine, the show promised to be a winner.

But as mentioned, the event wasn't to be called a *hot rod* show. Instead, the Slonakers selected the word *roadster*, for a very good reason. Says Mary Slonaker today, "At the time, hot rods were looked upon as an oddity. The name 'hot rod' was taboo." Furthermore, Al Slonaker realized the value of good publicity, and when the local newspapers told him that they wouldn't print stories about his automotive exhibition if it were called a hot rod show, the decision to call it a roadster show was settled.

In hopes of gaining editorial support—and free publicity—from the local press, the Slonakers agreed: the words "hot rod" were out, and the word "roadster" was in. So it was, the first official hot rod show at Oakland was to be the National Roadster Show. The date was January 19–22, 1950.

Hot Rod magazine (*they* had no reservations about using the term hot rod!) immediately jumped on the bandwagon, and offered editorial space to publicize the forthcoming show. First reference to the show appeared in the October 1949 issue of *Hot Rod*, and the Slonakers bought a two-page advertisement for the January 1950 issue to coincide with the event itself. The ad read, in part, "World's Fastest on Display. National Roadster Show. Oakland, California. January 19–22."

Within the advertisement's copy was the following: "Owners of roadsters in the Northern California area are confident of providing fine equipment that will challenge the best of cars from other sections of the country. According to Show Director Al Slonaker, a beautiful eight-foot trophy will be awarded to the most beautiful roadster displayed in the show." And so was born the title, "America's Most Beautiful Roadster," an award that lives on today, and is regarded as the crown jewel of the custom car show circuit.

Interestingly, the AMBR trophy grew another foot between the time the advertisement appeared in *Hot Rod* and the show was staged. But that's another story (see chapter 6). In fact, there are hundreds, even thousands of stories about Oakland that await. Space and time will not allow a recital about each and every one of them, but a brief look back at the show's first 50 years is in order. What follows on these pages are highlights and changes that have taken place at hot rodding's Granddaddy car show, the Grand National Roadster Show. Who would have thought that such a tiny car show would one day blossom into the mighty event that it has become today?

1950–1959
The Formative Years

Once show promoters Al and Mary Slonaker determined that the centerpiece for their 1950 Oakland auto show would be hot rods rather than new and foreign cars, they faced the next hurdle: corralling enough hot rods to make a worthy event. After all, if you are going to stage a hot rod show, then you must have an abundance of hot rods for the spectators to view and enjoy.

The 1949 hot rod exhibit was, by all rights, a fluke, considering that before the show the Slonakers knew absolutely nothing about these hybrid autos called hot rods. By the end of that first show, however, the enterprising show promoters had gained valuable insight into this form of motorsport. In the process, the young Bay Area couple also managed to establish a foothold within the local hot rod community itself. And so for the next several months the Slonakers started gathering the pieces necessary for what was to be the inaugural National Roadster Show.

The first order of business was to get the word to the local hot rodders, informing them that *they* would be the guests of honor—not the foreign car manufacturers—at the Exposition Building in 1950. To do that, the Slonakers literally took their message to the streets. Recalls Mary Slonaker nearly 50 years later about the couple's endeavors, "Al and I went to all the local places

Oakland, 1956, Richard Gray of Alameda, California, showed his '32 Ford three-window coupe. The top was chopped four inches, and the '54 Chrysler Red paint contrasted well with the white frame and running gear. The chrome wheels were a product of Don Hentzell, Western Wheel & Rim Co. A '48 Mercury engine was set back 25 percent. The Merc motor had a Potvin cam and four carbs. It set record speeds at Lodi, California, of 107 miles per hour. I wonder if that's Gray sitting on the front tire?

The first-ever National Roadster Show was held at the Oakland Exposition Building on January 19–22, 1950. This overhead shot shows the Oakland Clutch Busters Club display. The roadster in the foreground belonged to Ken Fuhrman of Berkeley. His '29 A body rests on a chromed '32 Ford frame. A specially crafted clear Plexiglas hood shrouds a souped-up '40 Mercury flathead. The fifth roadster to the far left was Gordon Vann's 1917 Dodge body on a '32 Ford frame. It, too, has a Mercury flathead V-8. Its unusual grille comes from a DeSoto. The front has a chromed custom nerf bar with a "V" initial. *Ken Fuhrman*

(malt shops, drive-ins, speed shops, etc.) where the hot rodders would hang out. We'd talk with them, ask them how they felt about a hot rod show."

Indeed, the Slonakers were so intent on making the next show a success that they became totally consumed by its genesis. As Mary points out, "Whenever we'd see one (a

In 1947 Ken Fuhrman was able to purchase this roadster for $100. A lot of money at that time! He removed the fenders and eventually put in a '46 Mercury engine that was bored to 3 5/16 inches and stroked 1/8 inch. Taking his frame and pieces to Oakland Chrome Platers, his roadster eventually appeared like this for the 1950 Roadster Show. *Ken Fuhrman*

hot rod) on the street, we'd pull him (the owner) over and tell him about our show." Posters were made, flyers handed out, and the Slonakers even contacted the local press, assuring them that the words "hot rod" would not appear in the show's promotional material as originally dictated by the media's administrators.

The seed had been planted, and like industrious farmers, the Slonakers diligently tended to their crop. The harvest would come January 19–22, 1950, when the doors finally opened at the Exposition Building in Oakland for the first-ever National Roadster Show.

Additionally, the Slonaker's man-on-the-street research told them that there would be a large contingent of circle-track racing roadsters entered (36 were ultimately listed in the show's first program) as well as the expected array of street rods (although that term had yet to be coined by the budding hot rod fraternity). Given those facts, Al Slonaker again showed his genius as a promoter by featuring one of the West Coast's more popular and well-known roundy-round race car drivers on the event souvenir program's cover (price for the program, by the way, was 25 cents). Posing alongside the behemoth nine-foot trophy to be presented to the recipient of the America's Most Beautiful Roadster award was Northern California's own Freddie Agabashian, a midget and sprint car driver who would later race in the Indianapolis 500 (earning the coveted pole position in 1952). Realizing, too, that it never hurts to have a pretty face in the picture, Slonaker included one more draw for the program's cover—Miss California. So, standing on the other side of the spectacular trophy was the flaxen-haired beauty, Jone Pedersen.

Interestingly, the show program listed the trophy as standing eight feet tall. Stated the cover caption inside, "Introducing Jone Pedersen, Miss California of 1949 and Freddie Agabashian, Northern California's favorite race driver. This pair will act as Host and Hostess for the National Roadster Show. The eight-foot trophy will be presented to the winning car of the show."

By the time Bill NieKamp's track-nose 1929 Ford was presented the AMBR trophy at the conclusion of the 1950 show, somebody in the Exposition Building must have measured the loving cup again, and determined it to be a foot taller than originally publicized. In his show report for *Hot Rod* magazine (March 1950), Griff Borgeson wrote, "And, as though to prove that hot rod maturity is here to stay, first prize—a handy nine-foot golden cup—was carried off by William Nie Kamp (sic) of Long Beach . . ."

As you might suspect, it was Al Slonaker who prescribed the dimensions for the AMBR trophy in the first place. In step with his typical P. T. Barnum way of promoting things, Slonaker realized that to make his National Roadster Show truly a sensation on the automotive community's event calendar, he'd have to do something really

The Salinas Hi-Timers club was represented at the 1950 show. Members from left to right are Mitch Steenhoudt, Joe Pistoni, Bill Cook, and Nick Reynal. Reynal owned this chopped and channeled '32 Ford three-window coupe, painted white with metallic brown scallops. A powerful '48 Mercury flathead turns the coupe around 103 miles per hour at the drag races. *Nick Reynal*

special. Thus, the nine-foot-tall loving cup that literally stood head and shoulders above all other trophies at the time. The trophy was later insured for $5,000.

His wife, Mary, wasn't as confident about investing so much money into a single trophy. Besides, she questioned, did anybody really have a trophy case big enough to fit a nine-footer? Looking back today on Al's decision to present such a huge trophy, Mary says, "I thought he (Al) was out of his mind."

Al held firm, explaining to his wife, "If they (the winner) had a business, that's what they'd want." His reasoning was simple: chances were good that the winner would either have a business, or access to a business that sponsored or helped build the winning hot rod roadster, so a Godzilla-size trophy would make an eye-catching display for shop customers during the 12-month period leading up to the next show. In fact, years later one of the AMBR winners and a

future promoter of the show, Don Tognotti, explained that after he won the trophy he displayed it in his father's automotive shop that, conveniently, had a 10-foot-high ceiling.

Based on attendance figures and *Hot Rod* magazine's show report, the four-day 1950 show was a huge success, drawing in 27,624 spectators. Wrote Borgeson for America's premier hot rod journal, "There were exactly 100 cars in the show, some from far-flung corners of the country, but No. Calif. cars were naturally most numerous, with So. Calif. jobs highly plentiful. As proof of the fairness of the judging, So. Calif. creations won the most awards. This was in spite of the fact that due to the geography involved, most of the judges were local men."

Oddly, the inaugural event nearly turned out to be the *only* National Roadster Show to be held in Oakland. According to Borgeson's report, the Slonakers had cast their collective eye on a show site across the bay for the

I took this picture in Oakland in 1973, when Jim "Jake" Jacobs of Temple City, California, showed his restored '29 Ford roadster, which won the title America's Most Beautiful Roadster in 1950. The car was originally built by William A. NieKamp of Long Beach, California. A Model A body sits on a '27 Essex frame, and had a '42 Ford engine. NieKamp was a member of the Southern California Timing Association.

second annual roadster bash. Wrote Borgeson at the end of his show report: "The 1951 National Roadster Show, according to present plans, is scheduled for sometime next January at San Francisco's Civic Auditorium. Producer Al Slonaker hopes to provide ample space for exhibiting an even larger group and a great selection of cars in the 1951 show."

Of course, history proves that the show remained in Oakland, becoming a fixture on that city's entertainment calendar for the next 47 years. Ironically, the show migrated across the bay for the 49th annual running in 1998 when the Oakland Coliseum management canceled the arena's car show dates for that year. And so, for its 49th year running, the Grand National Roadster Show was a San Francisco treat.

In any case, the 1951 show—held again in Oakland at the Exposition Building—went as planned, and was even expanded to six days, February 20–25. The new dates took advantage of George Washington's Birthday, which was celebrated separately in those days from Lincoln's Birthday (February 12).

By now, the Slonakers had a better handle on what their show would include and how they would run it. Again, the roadsters would be displayed in the old armory building at Exposition Hall, where the show remained every year until 1968 when the show would relocate to the newly built Coliseum, a huge sports complex that accommodated Oakland's major sports teams, including the major league baseball team the Oakland Athletics and the NBA Golden State Warriors. More than the previous year, the AMBR trophy commanded center stage in 1951, as Slonaker instructed the floor crew to direct 27 spotlights toward the loving cup that stood regally on the show floor.

Furthermore, the program's "Welcome!" message by show management clearly stated the purpose of the show, which was "to better acquaint the general public with the activities and products of roadster sportsmen."

There was also a degree of red, white, and blue American pride in the welcome message. The management—in the form of the Slonakers—jingoistically wrote in the program, "When you look at the Honor Roll on the stage and see how many are already serving in the armed

The San Francisco Ramblers club participated in many Oakland shows. Here, some of the club members gather for a picture, taken in April 1952 at McLaren Park, San Francisco. From left are Ron Tehany and friend, Fred Chiesa, Bud Crackbon (AMBR winner 1952), Ron Fulmer, Fred Zaft (Kneeling), Verne Brink, Henry Laurient and friend, Bud Jones, Terry Code, and Jack Dyer. *Ken Fuhrman*

Don Reid of Salinas, California, was one of the first car guys I met when I came to town in 1955. In 1953 Reid entered his chopped-top '41 Ford coupe, with fadeaway fenders in the Oakland Show. The paint was chrome yellow lacquer. Front end modifications include frenched headlights and custom grille. A modified flathead engine turned the coupe a flat 90 miles per hour at Salinas Drags. *Don Reid*

forces of the United States, you may appreciate the worth of these men—in war as well as peace." Page four of the program even listed each and every member of the local roadster clubs and SCTA who had recently joined the armed forces (remember, the Korean War had been under

Blackie Gejeian of Fresno, California, has been telling his famous story for years about how at the Oakland Roadster Show he drained the gas and oil from his Model T, removed the right-side hubcaps, then lifted the roadster onto its side so that spectators could walk around and see all the chrome underneath. Quite a spectacular feat for 1953, as Blackie demonstrated after the show. *Blackie Gejeian*

way for about a year during that time). Clearly, the message was more than just that hot rodders were common, friendly people; they also were loyal Americans.

The second show enjoyed a moment of "divine intervention," as well. In an effort to help legitimize the sport of hot rodding with the general public, the Slonakers managed to enlist the support of the local police chief, Lester J.

In 1953 Blackie Gejeian entered his '27 T roadster. An unidentified CHP officer presented him a participant trophy. The engraving read, "National Roadster Show, 1953, Oakland, Originality—Rod Construction, Third Place." Painted jet black, Blackie's roadster had cool-looking black and white Naugahyde upholstery, lots of chrome and a hopped up 296-ci Mercury engine. Blackie states the same roadster will be at the 50th anniversary show in 1999. Notice the roadster in back of Blackie's, it's Frank Rose's '27, the AMBR for 1954. *Frank Livingston*

In 1953, Joe Bailon of Hayward, California, showed his '41 Chevy custom coupe named *Miss Elegance*. Many modifications made this car special, including chopping the top 3 inches, filling the quarter windows, extending the rear windows around the side to give a hardtop effect, putting air scoops in the hood, forming a tube grille, and reshaping front fenders with frenched headlights. The hubcaps were made from a farmer's plow discs and cut down to fit 16-inch wheels. Bailon's paint color was maroon with gold iridescence. *Joe Bailon*

Sunday, February 22, 1953: California Highway Patrol (CHP) Officer Ezra Ehrhardt proudly presents the "Car of Elegance for 1953" award to a young Joe Bailon for his custom *Miss Elegance* '41 Chevy coupe. Notice the size of the trophy back then! Judging was based on construction and beauty. Only exhibitors could vote, however, they could not vote in the class that they had entered. By 1953 spectators could vote for "The People's Choice Award." *Frank Livingston*

Divine. In his opening statement celebrating the show's six-day presence in the city, Chief Divine stated, "The Oakland Police Department recognizes and appreciates the efforts of these men to curb reckless driving on the highways and to keep unsafe equipment off the streets."

Divine's published statement continued, "All of the men and organizations represented in the National Roadster Show are to be commended for the fine work they do. It is their spirit and knowledge that is so necessary to the nation in both peace and war."

Another 1953 CHP presentation, this one to Tom Hocker of Oakland, California. Ironically, Hocker was a member of the Kustoms of Los Angeles Club, winning in custom coupe class. This '40 Ford coupe has a chopped top, with fenders molded to the body, and side trim moldings removed. The engine is a 274-ci Mercury, with a Kong ignition. The interior is gray antique and white Naugahyde. The paint is Purple Sypho organic lacquer. *Frank Livingston*

This '49 Mercury chop-top coupe was owned by Bill Chatham of Alameda, California. The coupe was completely molded with electric doors and trunk. The headlights were frenched, and the taillights are from a '50 Buick. The grille came from a '46 Lincoln, and the '51-style fender skirts were louvered. The body was painted maroon, the interior upholstered with black and tan Naugahyde. Under the hood rests a modified '46 Mercury! Another fine custom for 1953. *Frank Livingston*

Left
Perhaps the most outstanding feature to Bailon's *Miss Elegance* was its chrome-plated dash built entirely of sheet stock. Bailon gifted it with 15 working gauges and 32 push buttons. In addition to a radio, it has a built-in cocktail bar. The hood, doors, trunk, ashtray, seats, and gas tank are all push-button operated from the dash. The upholstery is maroon velvet velour. This dash was one of a kind! *Frank Livingston*

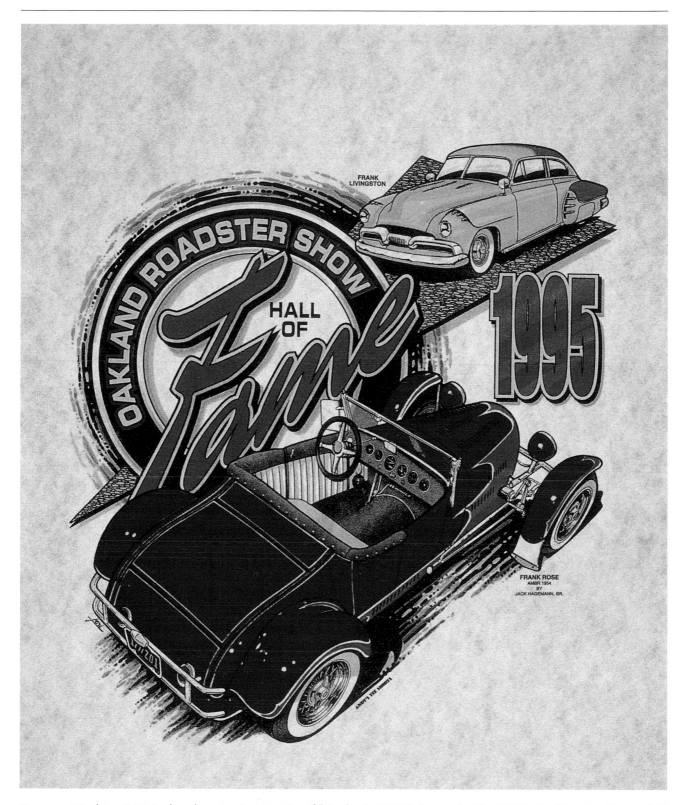

FRANK LIVINGSTON

HALL OF Fame

OAKLAND ROADSTER SHOW

1995

FRANK ROSE
AMBR 1954
BY
JACK HAGEMANN, SR.

To represent Frank Rose's '27 Ford roadster, America's Most Beautiful Roadster in 1954, I photographed the 1995 Oakland Roadster Show Hall Of Fame 17-inch x 22-inch felt poster. Rose's car was a one-of-a-kind roadster from the 1950s. Under its Jack Hagemann Sr. custom hood sat a 257-ci Ford V-8. The body included fenders and a hand-formed aluminum belly pan. Also appearing on this poster is Frank Livingston's custom '49 Chevy. Every year the Hall of Fame poster features past winners from Oakland. With these posters readers can appreciate the vibrant colors that have made the Oakland Show among the greatest in the world.

Sunday evening, February 28, 1954, National Roadster Show manager Mary Slonaker presents a trophy to Arthur "Red" Jones of Niles, California, for his *Jones Special*. The dragster was powered by a 316-ci Mercury flathead packed with a Howard M14 cam, Weiand quadruple carburetion, and Harmon and Collins Magneto. The suspension is torsion-bar type. The dragster turned 126 miles per hour in the quarter-mile drags. *Frank Livingston*

This full custom convertible at the 1954 Roadster Show belonged to Leon Welmas of Palm Springs, California. His '52 Chevy had a custom chopped-top with a one-piece windshield, and was lowered four inches in the true tradition. Headlights were frenched, and the hood and trunk were shaved clean. Taillights were Buick, frenched. The paint was metallic bronze and the upholstery white and bronze Naugahyde. *Frank Livingston*

Another interesting addition to the second show was what the promoters termed the "Theme Girl," which actually was a more politically correct (no, *that* phrase hadn't been adopted yet) way of saying "trophy queen." In any case, the first official Theme Girl was also a hometown girl, Miss Greta Groth. As it turned out, the Theme Girl title was warmly accepted by the show participants and spectators, and for the next few years Theme Girl it was.

By 1952 the National Roadster Show was recognized as the premier hot rod car show in America. The third annual show gave rise to another landmark event at Oakland. This was the show in which an aspiring customizer named Joe Bailon debuted his famous dashboard that formed the centerpiece for his 1941 Chevy custom, *Miss Elegance.* Bailon entered the '41 Chevy in the show, even though the bodywork and paint had not yet been completed. When Slonaker heard about the glitz-and-glitter dashboard, he called Bailon right away and told him to get the car in the armory building, no matter what. The following year Bailon returned with the car in finished form, and promptly drove away at the end of the show with the Custom d'Elegance Award in hand.

Miss Elegance's dashboard was, to say the least, spectacular, with chrome and gauges splashed across its uniquely formed metal surface. The instrument panel served as command central for no less than 15 gauges, 32 push buttons, a hand-built steering column, and a built-in cocktail bar! Bailon, who, through the years was instrumental in the completion of nine customs that would win the Custom d'Elegance Award (for top custom at the show), spent $1,160—a princely sum in the early 1950s—to build the dashboard. Today, he says, "it would take me $10,000 to duplicate that dashboard." Now, nearly 50 years later, the custom car world—and Bailon himself—may find out exactly how much it will cost to duplicate that fabled dashboard, because the Northern California customizer recently recovered his old dash from a salvage yard and has plans to build a second *Miss Elegance* (the original car was sold as scrap by a subsequent owner who, obviously, didn't appreciate or understand the car's worth as a historic collectible). Bailon will install the original dash, resplendent with new gauges and chrome, in the second edition of *Miss Elegance.*

Actually, a review of the entry list from the first roadster show reveals that there were several of today's legends who could be spotted at Oakland's Exposition Hall during that weekend. Leading the list were the Barris brothers, Sam and George, who entered a custom convertible at the 1950 show. The program for that year described the car, "Entered by Barris Kustom Shop of Bell. Buick and

Cadillac body with '47 Buick motor. Molded with body sections hammered. Everything push buttoned."

Gordon O. Vann, a local car builder who was destined to be one of the charter members for the GNRS Hall of Fame that was started in 1960, also entered an unusual roadster at the first show. He showcased a hot rod with a 1917 Dodge body perched atop a 1932 Ford frame. The clean-looking roadster had a DeSoto grille and was powered by a Mercury flathead V-8 engine. The interior was trimmed with, as the program described it, "Unborn Calf skin upholstery."

Other notable names at the first show included Ken Fuhrman (who also would join the Hall of Fame in 1997), speed wizard and cam specialist Howard Johansen (who entered his unique tandem-body streamline Bonneville racer that had been clocked at 171 miles per hour), Lee Chapel (builder of the gorgeous Lee's Speed Shop streamliner),

Here are three Grand National Roadster Show programs. To the left is the very first one, dated 1950. It's in mint condition, and is part of Bruce Heather's collection. The middle one is from 1990 and was titled "Entry List," and the one on the right is from 1998.

A fine example of a rod sedan at the '54 Show, it belonged to Ron Ortland from Orinda, California. Ortland was a member of the Walnut Creek Road Knights car club. His '40 Ford Tudor sedan was metallic green lacquer, with a louvered hood punched 92 times. Taillights were '41 Buick. The interior was trimmed in flat white Naugahyde. Under the hood rested a '46 Mercury engine with a dual-carb Offenhauser manifold, Weber cam, lightened flywheel, and Harmon and Collins ignition. Dig those wide whitewalls! *Frank Livingston*

and Rico Squalglia (who would win rights to the coveted nine-foot AMBR trophy the following year with his handsomely rebuilt '24 Ford).

To be sure, the early Oakland shows helped initiate many legendary hot rodders into the sport. Among them was a young man named Spence Murray, who, in the 1960s, would become editor of *Rod & Custom* magazine. Through his association with the show as a magazine editor, Murray formed a close relationship with the Slonakers. In a special 20th anniversary story about Oakland that he wrote for *R&C* (April 1968), Murray waxed nostalgic about his first time at the show. He wrote:

"Your editor, hardly dry behind the years, got wind of Oakland in time to take in the '52 show. At hand was a chopped '49 Chevy two-door. The show needed customs to help fill out that class, so I made the trek (the first of 17!) and humbly pitted the Chev against the likes of Joe Bailon and Sam and George Barris. With trophies only going down three places, our surprise was great to find we'd copped 2nd—behind Bailon but ahead of the Barris Brothers. Today that trophy, all 12 inches of it!, is the pride of my collection—the hardest won of them all."

Within a few years of the first show, Oakland had tapped the imagination of and kindled a spark of enthusiasm

In 1955, Blackie Gejeian of Fresno, California, was co-winner of the prestigious "America's Most Beautiful Roadster" award. He shared the award with Ray Anderegg and his T roadster. The show's Theme Girl, Mary O'Brien, hands Blackie a participant trophy at the awards presentation held Sunday, February 27. Blackie's name also was engraved on the big nine-foot trophy along with Ray Anderegg's name. *Frank Livingston*

This picture of Blackie Gejeian's 1955 AMBR winner was actually taken in 1956. Even so, it gives you a bird's-eye view and feeling of what it's like to sit behind the roadster racing-type steering wheel of a 1950s hot rod. Can you imagine Blackie reaching down and speed-shifting the chromed gear shift lever while the wind blows wildly through his hair and the smell of burnt rubber drifts through the air behind him? Sounds like a wild ride, doesn't it?

among the hot rod and custom car communities. To enter and show your car at the National Roadster Show was akin to qualifying for the Indianapolis 500. Soon car clubs from across the nation were submitting entries or encouraging their members to do whatever they could to get their hot rods on the show floor at the Exposition Hall in Oakland.

Leading the list of car clubs—as you might guess—was the Oakland Roadster Club. Other memorable club names that frequented the show during the 1950s included the San Francisco Ramblers, Speed Shifters (Hayward), Heaven Pacers (East Bay), Accelerators (Concord), King Pins (Oakland), Road Runners (San Mateo), Bay Area Customs, Satan's Angels Customs (Castro Valley), Ace High (San Mateo), Shifters (San Francisco), Idlers (Oakland), Swanx (Oakland), Studs Auto Club (Oakland), Poor Boys (San Francisco), Cam Shafters (Lafayette), Rod Benders (Hayward), and Thunderbolts (Sacramento), among others. Of course, there were dozens more in California alone, but these were among

the first clubs to participate at the custom car show.

As the number of entries grew, so did the number of trophies and class awards. By 1955 the trophy table was awash with more than 50 trophies to be distributed among the winners and runners-up in 20 divisions. In addition, there were three grand prizes that climaxed the traditional awards ceremony on Sunday night at the conclusion of the show. The three big awards were for America's Most Beautiful Roadster (of course!), Custom Car d' Elegance (to the top custom car), and The People's Choice (to the entry voted favorite by the spectators).

The trophy presentation spawned another deep-rooted tradition at Oakland—Move Out Night. As unique as the nine-foot AMBR trophy, Move Out Night is like no other final-night ceremony held by any other car show, for within a matter of minutes the entire show hall erupts into a frenzy of exhaust noise as internal combustion engines are fired up so that the show cars can—and must—be driven out on their own power.

In 1955, when Ray Anderegg of Merced, California, shared the title with Blackie Gejeian, his roadster was painted yellow and had a modified Mercury flathead V-8 engine. This picture shows Anderegg's roadster as it appeared in the 1991 Oakland Show, painted red with a contrasting white vinyl upholstery, sporting a 350 Chevy engine and a new license plate that reads, "AMBR 55."

This unusual '32 Ford five-windowed coupe belonged to Mervyn Toynton of San Francisco, California. Toynton's coupe, shown here at the 1955 Oakland show, was sectioned four inches through the grille shell, hood, quarter panel, doors and rear window. Note the one-piece top hood with louvered side panels. All the body-work and painting was done by R.C.H. Auto Body, and the pinstripes were applied by none other than Tommy the Greek. The coupe had '40 Ford hydraulic brakes all around, and the '40 Ford V-8 engine was equipped with Offenhauser heads and dual carbs. *Frank Livingston*

San Franciscan LeRoy French owned this full custom '49 Plymouth sedan. French was a member of the Shifters club of San Francisco. The top was chopped 4 1/2 inches in the front and 6 1/2 inches in the rear. Other custom tricks include frenched headlights, molded-and-louvered hood and trunk, floating grille from a '53 Oldsmobile, and frenched '49 Ford taillights. The engine was unique, even for its time—a 3/4-race Plymouth six cylinder. Paint was Bahama Blue lacquer. *Frank Livingston*

Once again the show's Theme Girl, Mary O'Brien, presents a trophy to LeRoy French, the young owner of this full custom. All the chroming on the Plymouth was done by C & M Plating of San Francisco. Jim Dunn did all the body work and painting at J. E. French Co. It was unusual then, as now, to have a four-door sedan as a custom car. Notice how the crowd took interest in the trophy presentation and the Theme Girl. *Frank Livingston*

This color picture of Ted Leventhal's custom '50 Chevrolet convertible was taken in 1956. It was taken specifically because of the unique custom front end. The hood was nosed off and peaked, with the hood corners rounded. Headlights were frenched and deep tunneled, the grille was hand-made from chromed copper tubing and sheet metal. Directional signals were made from translucent green plastic. Mel Pinoli painted the car bronze lacquer. Notice that the bumper bolts were smoothed off.

Much has been written and said about Move Out Night, but perhaps Spence Murray's description in his 20th anniversary story for *Rod & Custom* says it best:

"And that final Sunday night. THAT you have to see. In the old days when there were two categories of cars—just plain rods and customs—trophies went to 1st, 2nd, and 3rd places in the two divisions. That's all except, of course, for the Big One. Competition was never so keen as a half-hundred roadster owners sweated *that* out. But now Slonaker has had to bend somewhat with the times and the cars—still primarily rods and customs—are divided into a dozen or more classes and trophies are given far down in each pack. Still, the crowds pour back in on that final day to see who wins what and to hear the roar as, after the presentations, the cars are fired up and driven out of the hall. Yes, we said *driven!* To our knowledge no other show allows cars to be run during the show, especially when the place is packed with sev-

eral thousand bystanders. But then, Oakland is different, and this is part of what makes it so. Dragster engines, custom car engines, funny car engines, and (who could forget) roadster engines—it's enough to rattle the ears and the eyes water as exhaust fills the room. There's the tire-screeching dash for the few exits, the trophy-losers mad at everyone and in a hot-tempered rush to get out (but they'll be back next year, they always are). Fists have been bared at Oakland, and probably will be again, but the judge's word is final and no decisions can be altered."

Concluded Murray, "In the wee hours of Monday they're all gone. Paper cups by the thousands lie flattened on the floor. The tensel [sic] of car displays lies heaped and dirty. There's still the smell of exhaust, but it's as quiet as a tomb. Soon, the work crews will begin the mammoth task of restoring the exhibit hall and taking down the banners. Another grandaddy [sic] of them all, the unforgettable

Left
Ted Leventhal's '50 Chevy modified custom convertible was a winner in '55. The show's Theme Girl, Martha O'Brien, presented Leventhal with the gold. Leventhal was a member of the Satan's Angels Customs of Oakland. His car was lowered all around, and the body completely molded. Doors and trunk were operated electrically. The custom's design and bodywork were done by Emery Robinson. Mel Pinoli sprayed the Tropic Green iridescent and white lacquer paint. The interior was green with white piped Naugahyde. *Frank Livingston*

Next Page
I originally took black and white pictures of the late Eddie Bosio's '32 Ford roadster in 1956 at the Monterey Kar Kapades. Years later, 1969 to be precise, I took this color picture. Eddie won the AMBR title in 1956. During the early days of hot rodding the roadster belonged to Vic Edelbrock Sr. Later Bosio named the roadster *Mr. Ed.* The highboy roadster features special front fenders, a curved windshield, special chromed header pipes, and nerf bars front and rear. It had a 284-ci Mercury flathead engine with all the Edelbrock accessories. Orange and white pinstriping and paint was applied by Tommy the Greek.

By 1956 it was prevalent that the pinstriping craze was about to become very fashionable. Not seeing many cars striped before, I had to take a picture of this '32 Ford coupe grille shell with red and black stripes. The pattern really wasn't very symmetrical. The coupe's white paint was also unique. Later I found the color white was becoming popular. Bob Mailho of Lafayette, California, and a member of the Accelerators of Concord, owned the coupe. Its drivetrain consisted of a 276-ci Mercury V-8, '39 Ford transmission, and a Halibrand quick change rear end.

Oakland, 1956: Harry Love Jr. of Redwood City, California, owned this '32 Ford highboy roadster. It was painted the ever popular bright red lacquer, with red and white Naugahyde upholstery. Underneath the hood is a '48 Mercury, with Edelbrock heads and three-carb Evans manifold. The early Ford transmission has Lincoln gears and the rear end is a '34 Ford. Harry told me when he entered the car in the show that it was not completely finished. Later I asked him, "Where are your taillights?"

Oakland Roadster Show, has come and gone. But somewhere someone is already preparing for the next one—or perhaps the one after that. Can't let the 'Big One' get away."

Not all of Oakland's traditions have been successful, though. There have been a few flops, among them the Rhoda Award. The Rhoda was derived from the show's roadster theme. The Slonakers originally intended the Rhoda to be as important to Oakland winners as an Academy Award is to the movie industry. When reminded of the Rhoda Award,

Oakland, February 25, 1956. This '32 Austin Bantam coupe was originally built by Rudy Kershing of Salinas, California, with a 235-ci Wayne Chevy. Paint was red and yellow. The new owner, Art Balliet of San Francisco, had Tommy the Greek repaint the coupe in the Pacers' car club colors. Later the engine was changed to a Mercury flathead. Notice the style of the Moon spun aluminum wheel discs. As you can see, flame painting was even popular back then!

Here is another overall shot taken at the 1956 show. In the background behind Ray Anderegg's 1955 AMBR co-winner you can see the nine-foot tall AMBR trophy. On other side of the trophy sits Blackie Gejeian's '27 roadster. The rear view of the T roadster to the right belongs to Jerry McKenzie, who came all the way from Indiana. The driver's view of the dragster in the foreground is J. E. Riley & Son's, driven by Cal Rice, which clocked 143.95 miles per hour with its 331-ci Chrysler.

This picture shows Robert Rosen's chopped and channeled '32 Ford competition coupe at the 1956 show. Rosen was a member of the Hayward Head Hunters club. With the hood panels up you can see how the Oldsmobile engine was moved back 26 inches. It was estimated to produce 300 horsepower on gas. The racer was painted yellow with black striping. The '29 roadster belongs to B'Ho Kirkland and Dick Bonvicino. It has a 300-ci Mercury with Edelbrock heads and manifold, and a Potvin cam. For improved traction the engine was set back in the frame. It held Valley Timing Association drag and dry lake speed records.

Mary Slonaker today candidly says, "We tried that, and it didn't work out too well. It was supposed to be like the Oscars, but it went over with a dull thud."

Actually, the Rhoda was intended to be a catch-all award to cover entries that didn't dovetail into any particular class or category. As the 1957 show program pointed out, "Rhodas are also awarded to special exhibits that defy classification." Which means, if an exhibit appeared on the show floor, and the promoters liked it well enough, then it deserved a Rhoda. The "dull thud" silenced the Rhoda forever, and once again a car or exhibit could win only if it had merit based on a particular criteria.

That first decade—the 1950s—was an exciting, even turbulent, time for hot rodding, for it was an era full of new and rich ideas being cast about by the customizers. To be sure, hot rodding was not new to the scene—car builders had been constructing what they called "soup jobs" or "bugs" as far back as the time the Model T was introduced in 1908—but it was during the initial 15 or so years after World War II that this form of motorsport really grew into its own element. As a result, new and unique techniques were tried and pioneered by early rodders. Some of those innovations succeeded, others failed. But no matter what the outcome of a building technique or fashion, it's important to note that it probably was prompted by shows such as the Oakland Roadster Show.

Perhaps one of the more notable advancements in the art of customizing cars was the introduction of candy apple paint, which hit the custom scene shortly after Oakland had established itself as an institution among car shows. For years painters had been trying to master the technique of giving paint the same tone and texture as the deep, translucent color found in a candy-covered apple you could buy at a carnival or state fair. Among the first car painters to hit on a candy apple formula that worked was Joe Bailon. The year was 1955.

Years later, Bailon says: "I wanted a color that would resemble the color of a taillight lens. You know, really shiny." To attain that "really shiny" look he experimented with all sorts of toners and translucent top coats. It helped paint companies, that by that time, were offering quality gold powders and metallic mixers to the toners. Naturally, Bailon tested them all.

"Finally," recalls the crafty painter and metalsmith, "fooling around on the (work) bench I tried a powder with Sherman-Williams maroon toner. That's how I stumbled on the candy color."

Bailon's first successful attempt at painting a show car with candy apple paint occurred when he sprayed Jerry Sahogon's '51 Chevrolet prior to the 1956 Oakland Show. "That was the first one," Bailon points out today.

Sahogon's was a typical Bailon custom, with a hand-formed front end, extended rear fenders capped with '55

To obtain this overall high angle shot I stood atop a corner aisle oil drum. The '32 Ford coupe to the left was George Sein's *Flamer*, built by Barris Kustoms. The car still exists, and is in Pueblo, Colorado. To the right, the bobbed '29 Ford roadster pickup with '53 Olds power belonged to Robert Sletton of San Rafael. To the rear is the Marin Coupe and Roadster club Crosley competition sedan, which ran at Bonneville in 1952 attaining 149 miles per hour. To the right rear is George Critchfield's full-fendered '32 Ford. The back part of the building had a display of the East Bay Pickups club.

DeSoto taillights and complemented with a '53 Oldsmobile rear bumper. A year later the car was entered in the '57 Oakland Show, and the program listed it as "lowered all around, special paint and color 'Candy Apple Red,' white interior. All work by Joe Bailon."

According to Bailon, that first candy apple paint job lost its luster prematurely, but with additional experimenting he touched on a formula that was able to stand up over time. Armed with the new formula, Bailon created the *Candy King* pickup custom later that year. "I worked on this one," he recalls. "It was *really* bright."

These and subsequent candy apple paint jobs helped earn Joe Bailon the title Mr. Candy Apple. But what many people don't realize today is that he was also responsible for one of the earliest flame paint jobs in hot rodding. It was on a 1929 Ford coupe that he built in 1938. Bailon was 16 years old at the time.

About the time that Bailon was busy experimenting with his candy apple colors, another young hot rod pioneer was gearing himself up to win the coveted nine-foot AMBR trophy. His name was Blackie Gejeian, a colorful character who hailed from nearby Fresno, California, a farming community smack in the middle of the San Joaquin Valley that

Through all my research, I could not find anything on this fabulous-looking '40 Ford coupe. It's too nice not to publish, so once again here's another white car from the 1956 Oakland Roadster Show. The orange grille and wheels with white pinstriping around the hub caps are very striking. The teardrop striping on the door and white exhaust headers look typically Tommy the Greek. the interior has chromed window moldings that accent the white Naugahyde upholstery. If anybody recognizes the coupe, please let me know.

In 1957 Dave Cunningham of San Francisco entered his '40 Ford Tudor sedan, which was channeled five inches. The fenders were molded to the body and the rear fender wells were radiused. Other custom work included taillights from a '41 Studebaker, and punching 58 louvers in the sectioned hood. The bumpers were from a '48 Ford, and the doors and trunk operated electronically. The interior had oxblood and ivory Naugahyde with a matching tarpaulin over the back seat. Dave's was one of the first—and finest—customs with a candy red paint job. The car is currently owned by Dick Falk, of Concord, California. *Bruce Heather collection*

With imagination and creativity, Joe Bailon of Hayward, California, came up with this '55 Chevy sedan that he customized into his own style pickup. The top rear cab panel came from a '40 Oldsmobile, and '37 Chevy fenders form the corners. Bailon painted his custom candy apple red, and the grille is special with chrome-plated letters advertising "Bailon." The bed had a tonneau cover, and the exhaust stacks protruded upward. Shown here is Dean Jeffries from Los Angeles pinstriping the truck in 1957. *Joe Bailon*

runs up the center of the state. Fresno also happened to be home for a small army of hot rodders and car customizers, so Blackie fit right in among this crowd.

The record book shows that Blackie, along with Ray Anderegg, was the first co-winner for the AMBR award. As it turned out in 1955, both Blackie's and Anderegg's cars tied in points, so the judges decided to let the two share the award. Interestingly, both roadsters were based on 1927 Fords (although Anderegg's started life as a coupe).

What the record books don't show about Blackie's car is that, like its owner, it had a colorful history leading up to the 1955 Oakland Show. "I raced it on the dry lakes in '47 and '48," says Blackie today, adding, "I crashed it real bad in '48." About that time the hot rodders on the West Coast were paying as much attention to how their cars looked as to how well they performed, so Blackie took a hiatus from the dry lakes racing to gussy-up his roadster. Blackie explains, "I rebuilt it into a show car." The first show he entered was Gene Winfield's 1949 event, held at a Ford dealership in Modesto, California.

On the evening of February 24, 1957, Dave Cunningham was presented with his class trophy. It was customary, and an honor, to receive it alongside your car. Usually, it was presented by the show's Theme Girl, an official of the show, or by a CHP officer. Doing the honors here is CHP Officer Bill Porter, congratulating Cunningham with a handshake and the trophy. Under magnification I saw Cunningham's name already engraved on the trophy for winning the Street Sedan Division. He sold the sedan in the mid-1960s. *Bruce Heather collection*

Through the grapevine Blackie heard about Slonaker's car show in Oakland. That was in 1949, and Blackie attended (but he didn't enter his car), and to this day claims that he has yet to miss an Oakland Roadster Show. Finally, he entered his roadster for a shot at the nine-foot trophy in 1953, losing to Dick Williams. The following year he lost again, prompting him to return home to Fresno for a third facelift for the Model T. As Blackie says about missing the mark the first two times: "I changed the whole goddamn car. Just to make a complete change, so that each time I went, the car was different."

Persistence paid off, and for 1955 he returned with the car's undercarriage all chromed and polished. That year he nicknamed the roadster *Chicken Coop* "because it was built in a chicken pen" on his family's property. *Chicken Coop* also was, as far as he knows, the first hot rod with a completely chromed undercarriage.

All that glistening chromed underware didn't go to waste, either. The spectators at Oakland in 1955 got to see Blackie's all-chrome underpinnings because he made sure they could see it. "We displayed the car on its side," he explains. "Every hour on the hour five of us lifted the car on its side, and balanced it on the side of the two wheels so people could see it (the chrome chassis)." To perform such a feat, Blackie drained all the coolant, gas and engine oil from the car prior to the show. The display obviously worked, and suddenly showmanship, as much as workmanship, became a part of Oakland's lore and agenda.

Late Sunday evening of February 24, 1957, after all the trophies were given out, two happy fellows show their gold. To the left, standing next to his '49 Chevy fastback, is Frank Livingston with his Crown America Grand Award: Semi-Custom Car d'Elegance. To the right is Joe Bailon, winner of the Full Custom Car d'Elegance, alongside his '55 Chevy pickup. *Joe Bailon*

Quoting the 1958 National Roadster Show program, "Day by day, see a roadster being built! On stage, to the front of the building, Romeo Palamides and his crew are building a roadster. The final night, the roadster will be taken off the stage, fired up and driven into the street." The finishing touch, of course, was pinstriping by the master, Tommy the Greek. The roadster happened to be Ken Fuhrman's '29 Ford. *Ken Fuhrman*

Indeed, Blackie was among the first hot rodders to capitalize on the benefits of showmanship. A few years after winning the AMBR, he promoted his own custom car show in Fresno, and to this day his show remains an integral part of the show circuit, being an invitation-only affair that showcases some of the finest hand-built cars in America.

But back to Oakland: During the latter part of 1957 leading up to the 1958 Oakland show, Blackie helped

Richard Peters, another member of the Fresno Moto Mafia, build what turned out to be one of the landmark AMBR winners—*Ala Kart*, a '29 Ford roadster pickup that broke new ground in hot rod construction. In truth, *Ala Kart* was a product of George Barris' shop, but Blackie and Peters were the prime movers behind the construction of its all-chrome chassis. As the car neared completion at Barris' shop down in Lynwood, California, Blackie and Peters worked round the clock to get all the running gear and suspension components plated and polished. Peters and Blackie endured all-night forays in which they'd drive to Barris' shop to deliver newly chromed parts, then hurry home for work the next day. "One stretch I went nearly three days without sleep," recalls Blackie.

The payoff was one heck of an undercarriage that was so striking Blackie couldn't bear to have it go unnoticed by the Oakland crowd. "I said to Peters, 'This thing is too beautiful not to show off.'" So Blackie had a plan, which led to the wild tale about how he originated the idea for putting mirrors beneath the car to give spectators a worm's-eye view of a show car.

The saga begins when Blackie found himself in the women's restroom (don't ask—we're talking about Blackie Gejeian, one of the most unforgettable characters hot rodding will ever experience) at the Oakland Exposition Building. As Blackie tells the story:

For those who participated in the early Roadster Shows, this 1959 view of Frank Monteleone's '56 Ford driving into the Exposition Building's parking lot entrance must bring fond memories! This is the building where it all began. Today the building is gone. Monteleone's car was built by Barris, painted Tingia Red and white. It was later featured on the cover of *Motor Life* and appeared in the film *Hot Car Girl*. *Bruce Heather*

"I knew there was a long mirror in the women's restroom, so I went in there to take it down. Some guy who worked at the show found me in there, and he said, 'What are you doing?' and I said 'What does it look like I'm doing, I'm taking down the mirror.' He said, 'You can't do that,' and I told him that I was only taking it down to see something. So the guy said 'Mr. Slonaker won't like this,' and he went to get Al. Al comes in while I'm removing the mirror from the wall and asks what I'm doing, and I tell him, 'I'll put it back, I promise.' " Realizing who he was dealing with, Slonaker shrugged his shoulders in resignation, then left the scene while Blackie slowly walked out onto the show floor with the unwieldy mirror balanced precariously in his arms.

Blackie and Peters gingerly placed the long mirror beneath *Ala Kart*, propping one side of the reflective glass so that a mirror-image of *Ala Kart*'s remarkable chromed chassis could be viewed from the aisle. Thus was born the first mirror display at a custom car show. (By the way, Blackie did as he promised, and returned the mirror to the ladies' restroom—but only after the nine-day show concluded and *Ala Kart* copped its first of two successive AMBR awards! As he put it years later, "They [the ladies at the show] didn't get to use that mirror all weekend. It was under the car.")

Up to the time *Ala Kart* carted away the big trophy in 1958, the winners of hot rodding's most-sought-after award had all been street-driven roadsters. *Ala Kart* was different. It was a dedicated show car, built for one purpose, and that was for show. Its bodywork consisted of grafting portions of '29 and '27 Ford pickup bodies together. The bed was completely hand-formed and fitted with custom trim to match the black-and-white rolled-and-pleated Naugahyde interior and removable soft top. The splash aprons were dressed with hand-formed louvers, and the nose piece was fashioned to resemble a track-T racer's. A pair of canted dual-headlights were molded into the grille shell's sides, and the fenders were bobbed and trimmed to enhance the truck's compact appearance. Finally, Barris had famed painter Dean Jefferies finish it with white pearl paint and gold-and-purple graphics.

Ultimately, *Ala Kart* helped usher in a whole new era for the National Roadster Show. The small-time builder was getting pushed to the side, and the AMBR was becoming the domain of a new breed of builder. The AMBR roadster candidates now were being carefully planned and built to score points toward the most prestigious award on the custom car show circuit. There would be a few more winners that maintained a connection with real-world hot rodding, but for the most part the days of the home-built roadster winning the AMBR were numbered. The Grand National Roadster Show was about to live up to its name, as some truly grand show cars were about to enter the scene.

Shown entering the building in 1959 is Richard Strock of Downey, California, with his chopped '32 Ford coupe. The coupe was also used in many movies and television shows. It was featured in *Drag Strip Girl*, *The Life Of Riley*, and in the *Dragnet* TV show. The engine was a chromed-plated Chrysler V-8. The interior is rolled and pleated in Air Foam and Natural Tan Naugahyde. Barris Kustoms built the coupe. *Bruce Heather*

The 1957 Roadster Show's program advertisement stated, "Craftsman Photographic Studio. Official show photographers. Frank Faraone and Bill Falkowich." Custom car guy and photographer Dave Cunningham took this picture of Frank Faraone in 1959 with camera bag on shoulder and Speed Graphic camera in hand. Theme Girl Linda Camara discusses how to pose for pictures with Mitch Nagao's custom '57 Ford Thunderbird. Some of Frank's pictures are in this book and I would like to acknowledge him and his talent! *Bruce Heather*

1960–1969
The Transitional Years

To truly appreciate the changes that took place within the Grand National Roadster Show's rank and file during the 1960s, it's necessary to understand and appreciate the goings-on among the rest of the world at that time, too. For never before in America's history had there been a decade with a more tumultuous and far-reaching effect on our society than the 1960s.

The 1960s saga began at the start of the decade when newly elected President John F. Kennedy made his extraordinary challenge for Americans everywhere to meet and explore what he termed the New Frontier. Among the many exceptional highlights of that most unforgettable decade were the following: three political assassinations (John F. Kennedy in 1963, Dr. Martin Luther King Jr., and Robert F. Kennedy in 1968); the escalation of an ill-conceived U.S. arms and troops build-up for the Vietnam War; war protesters supported by a militant antiwar movement (now there's an oxymoron!); hippies and yippies, and numerous other factional movements; Beatlemania and the origin of "acid rock"; free love, Haight-Ashbury and Woodstock; the return of a once-defeated national political figure (Richard M. Nixon) to the White House as president; and man's first step on the moon.

Dan Woods of Paramount, California, wanted something different, so he milked a fiberglass specialist for all he could about using the resin-based material, then set about building the *Milk Wagon*. This custom was no crate on wheels, either, and had a boxed '29 Ford frame with a single Corvair spring on homemade chromemoly dropped axle. The engine was a '57 Pontiac mill fed by six Stromberg 97 carbs on a classic Edelbrock manifold. The sleek custom headers use motorcycle baffles for mufflers. The pearl white and violet Metalflake was applied by Dan and Art Chrome Body Shop of Hollydale, California. The crew quarters was finished with lilac velvet diamond-tufted upholstery. In case you're wondering, the headlights were from a 1906 Reo.

From the 1950s to early 1960s, one particular outstanding roadster belonged to Ed Ducazau of Gardena, California. Ducazau was also a member of the Renegades of Long Beach car club. His '29 Ford roadster pickup body sits on a '32 frame. It was Cadillac powered, had a tuck-and roll interior, and featured lots of chrome on the front end, wheels and exhaust system. Beautiful burgundy paint.

Clearly, changes occurred at an exceptionally rapid rate during that era, due in large part to so many advancements in modern technology. For instance, television news reporting from Vietnam—in some instances including footage of the combat taking place in the rice paddies and jungles—became so efficient that Americans were able to witness from the comfort of their living rooms the death and destruction that war posed. Those same

Richard Peters' Barris-built *Ala Kart* was the AMBR winner for 1958 and 1959. It was displayed at the 1960 show but was not in competition for the AMBR award. *Ala Kart's* body was unique, being a combination of '29 and '27 Ford panels. The engine was a '54 Dodge equipped with Hilborn fuel injection and a Vertex magneto. The grille and nose piece were custom made, and the complete undercarriage was chrome plated. The roadster pickup was painted pearl white. The burgundy and gold streamers and pinstriping were applied by Dean Jeffries.

advancements in telecommunications technology allowed an awestruck world to witness live coverage of the first lunar walk; by the end of the decade the Moon—for centuries considered just another celestial body that man could only gaze at during quiet nocturnal hours—was now accessible. Indeed, by 1969 even color television—a

America's Most Beautiful Roadster of 1960 belonged to Chuck Krikorian of Fresno, California. Known as the *Emperor*, it was built by Krikorian and Barris with help from Blackie Gejeian. The '29 Ford body was channeled over a chromed Model A frame. Between the frame sat a Cadillac engine with all-chromed running gear. The Barris touch could be seen in the matching grille panel front and rear, and candy Magenta paint with pearl white Naugahyde interior. Blackie owns the car today.

This blue '30 Model A pickup belonged to Frans Scholin Jr. of Walnut Creek, California. The body was channeled over the frame, and the pickup bed made with birchwood. The top, tonneau cover, and interior were trimmed with white Naugahyde. It had a '56 Corvette engine for power. The candy apple red '27 roadster pickup was owned by Joe Schwede of San Mateo. It, too, had a '56 Chevy V-8 engine. The front and rear ends were chromed, as were the wire wheels and other accessories. White Naugahyde covered the interior, top and pickup bed. This photo was taken at the 1960 show.

This nice '32 Ford coupe was at the 1960 show. The Deuce coupe belonged to Bill Stanton of Concord, California. The engine under the louvered hood was a tri-power '53 Oldsmobile with H & C roller cam and chrome valve covers. The front end had a dropped axle with tube shocks. The transmission was typical early Ford, mating a '39 Ford transmission to a '48 Ford rear. The interior was brown and yellow Naugahyde, and the paint color was called Golden Yellow.

Louie Maze of Hayward, California, owned this '28 Ford roadster pickup, painted a beautiful blue metallic. He was a member of the Clutchmen club of Oakland. Under the louvered hood sat a 3/8-inch x 3/8-inch flathead engine with three carburetors. The interior was done in white and blue Naugahyde, and the running boards were upholstered in Naugahyde pleats. The wheels were chromed reversed '50 Mercury. A nice street rod, then and now!

Richard Guasco of Hayward, California, won AMBR in 1961 with his '29 Model A roadster on a '32 Ford frame. The engine is a 296-ci '57 Chevy, with Lincoln gears packed in a '36 Ford transmission. The '48 Ford rear end was modified with a quick change differential. Upholstered in pearl white Naugahyde, with silver-gray rugs, the car was striking with its pearl champagne orchid paint applied by Ortiz Customs.

Trophy night, 1961. "King of the Kustomizers" George Barris said a few words about the show crowd. Whenever Barris came to Oakland he always made a few comments on trophy night. The CHP Officer is unidentified, but at the extreme right in the photo, ready to strike a match to his cigarette, is the man who initiated the first show in Oakland back in 1949—Al Slonaker.

novelty when the 1960s began—could be found in many homes across America. The 1960s was certainly a decade of change for many Americans.

America's automotive culture didn't go untouched,

Award night, 1961. To the left is Bob Tindle of Portland, Oregon, getting a trophy for his *Orange Crate* '32 Sedan. The CHP officer remains unidentified, but next to him is Rich Guasco's mother, accepting the trophy for her son, who wasn't present because he had just been drafted into the army. Helping Mrs. Guasco is Joe Ortiz, of Ortiz Customs. Standing beside them is one of the Theme Girls for that year's show.

experiencing radical changes during that decade. Among the occurrences during that time was the realization by drag racers and Bonneville racers that jet engines offered exceptional performance boosts toward achieving greater top speeds; engineers designing cars for the Indianapolis 500 performed a flip-flop, moving the engine to the rear of the race car for improved handling; drag racing adopted a new word—Funnycar; and a place called Baja was on its way to becoming known as the world's longest unpaved speedway.

Radical change found its way into the National Roadster Show, too, and by the end of the decade the event's *modus operandi* had altered considerably. Even the name had been changed to *Grand* National Roadster Show in 1962. Today many Oakland historians trace the beginning of the show's metamorphosis to 1958 and 1959 when *Ala Kart* swept back-to-back AMBR honors. *Ala Kart* was so unique that, in essence, it raised the level of competition for the coveted nine-foot trophy to new heights. By 1960, builders realized that to win the cup, they'd have to dip deep into their well of creativity to beat the competition, and reach deep into their pockets to make it happen. When *Ala Kart* was built in 1957 it was worth a reported $17,000—lots of money in those days.

From Antioch, California, Thomas Jones entered his channeled '32 Ford coupe in the 1961 show. Maroon in color, with maroon and white piped Naugahyde upholstery, the car was a real eye-catcher. The engine that Thomas chose was a '56 Pontiac using three carburetors. The entire front end and wheels were chrome plated. Thomas was a member of the Bedouins auto club.

Ever since 1950 the Oakland Show's motto was, "Same time, same place, Granddaddy of all auto shows, the National Roadster Show! Come back Sunday night (February 26, 1961), see the awards ceremony, hear the roar of the engines and watch the cars leave the building." And that's exactly what they have been doing every year of the show. The first roadster, a '28 Ford, leaving the building in this photo belonged to Dave Dias. Behind him was Robert Curtin's '26 Model T.

Famous fiberglass customizer Bob McNulty, of Hayward, California, built this '57 Corvette for Bill Shelley of Oakland. The front of the Corvette has been extended several inches into a "V" shape, utilizing a grille from solid rod that was shaped to the grille opening. The canted headlights were from, of all things, an Edsel. Western Wheel & Rim Co., supplied the chromed reversed wheels. The paint is fine Metalflake silver, a popular treatment at the time. For contrast, the body was finished with purple scallops and white pinstripes.

Seeing the roadsters parked in the street outside the building, with the headlights illuminating each other, I decided to shoot another picture. To the left is Don Kugler's T roadster pickup. That's Kugler walking toward his roadster after conferring with Gary Kidwell in his channeled '32 Ford. Nothing beats Move Out Night at Oakland.

Yet, despite *Ala Kart*-owner Richard Peters' win-at-all-expense attitude, he remained an anomaly for Oakland in 1960: having won the AMBR trophy two years running, Peters—the first person to do so—elected not to vie for the AMBR trophy a third straight year. And so, when Peters wheeled *Ala Kart* into the Exposition Building for the 1960 National Roadster Show, he flew a flag of truce, declaring the legendary show car a neutral participant that would not compete for the big cup. Instead the famous pearl-white truck was proudly displayed on the floor of the Exposition Building for exhibition purposes only.

As it turned out, there was more than just a sense of brotherly love on Peters' part for this turn of events. You might say it was *brotherly-in-law* love that prompted Peters to voluntarily shine the spotlight away from *Ala Kart*, for it was Peters' brother-in-law, Chuck Krikorian, who had a roadster that certainly seemed worthy of winning the cup that year. By taking *Ala Kart* out of the picture, Krikorian stood an even better chance of winning in 1960.

Actually, Krikorian debuted his 1929 Ford roadster—dubbed *Emperor*, and, like *Ala Kart*, it was built by George Barris—the year before, but it was soundly beaten by Peters' truck. Regardless of which car won the AMBR that year, *Emperor* was every bit as elegant—in show car terms—as *Ala Kart*. It boasted a fully chromed undercarriage, a polished quick-change rear end, a spiffy 1958 Cadillac Eldorado engine, and a formed grille shell much on the same lines as *Ala Kart*'s. The channeled body was dressed with 30 coats of Burgundy Tangerine lacquer studded with diamond dust pearl impressions. Truly a magnificent car.

So it was that in 1960, with *Ala Kart* on the sidelines, *Emperor* was presented the big trophy. Consequently, for the third straight year, America's most beautiful roadster hailed from the rural city of Fresno, California. And the winner was yet another creation of the Barris shop in Los Angeles.

In 1963, this outstanding '30 Ford five-window coupe, owned by Ron Mancebo of Redding, California, featured a fully chromed chassis. Custom chrome nerf bars replace stock bumpers that help protect the '32 grille shell and radiator. The engine is a 276-ci '48 Mercury flathead with three carbs. The paint is royal blue and pearl white, with pearl white upholstery.

Northern California's East Bay Rods car club was in force at the '63 show. This beautiful '28 Ford roadster pickup belonged to Mike Morrison of Oakland. Powered by a 283-ci Chevy, it had a front end from a '34 Ford with a dropped axle; the rear was from a '48 Ford. Paint was Matador Red, matched with red and white Naugahyde upholstery. As a special touch, the running boards were chromed.

Bill Cushenbery's *Silhouette* premiered in 1963 at the San Mateo Autorama, just a month prior to this picture. The chassis is based on a shortened '56 Buick, with a '56 Buick engine. The sleek body was handmade by Cushenbery, with an Acry Plastics blown bubble top. Bill Manger stitched the Naugahyde interior, and Cushenbery applied the striking pearl lavender paint. That year Cushenbery was the first to win "Master Builder Award," which included a free trip to the Paris Auto Show with the Slonakers.

The following year the Earth's axis—so far as people at Oakland were concerned, anyway—shifted back to normal when a soft-spoken hot rodder from nearby Hayward, California, captured the cup with a rather sedate and straightforward street roadster based on a 1929 Ford. Richard Guasco built his Model A on a Deuce frame, basing the design on more traditional building methods and standards; a 283-ci Chevrolet small-block V-8 engine (bored to 296 ci) put its power through a 1936 Ford transmission packed with Lincoln Zephyr gears that spooled the reciprocating motion rearward to a 1948 Ford rear end equipped with a quick-change center. It was, in the eyes of the hot rod crowd, essentially all traditional speedware. Compared to either *Ala Kart* or *Emperor*, Guasco's Model A was a rather mild, even common-looking, hot rod. What caught the judges' attention was the workmanship that Guasco put into his roadster, and by voting his '29 top pick, the Oakland establishment made it clear once again that winning still required skilled execution, as much as

thoughtful implementation, of all the right parts.

Traditionalists breathed a sigh of relief at Guasco's AMBR win. And while they caught their breath, Barris regrouped in his shop. The establishment was in for another Barris treat, this time with The King of Kustomizers' own hot rod roadster.

In 1962 Barris threw his welder's hat in the ring for a shot at winning his own AMBR award. In a move to have his name officially inscribed on the trophy, Barris entered his own hot rod roadster, called *Twister T*; the owner, not the builder, gets official recognition, and for the three years that *Ala Kart* and *Emperor* won, Barris basked in the glory, although the inscription on the trophy didn't mention his name. He did, however, enjoy the just and deserved accolades showered upon him by the entire custom car and hot rod establishment for his genius and labors to this pair of fine AMBR winners.

In any case, in 1962 *Twister T* stormed into the Exposition Building and blew the competition away. As

This Model A roadster pickup was a joint venture between Frank Thaxter and Bill Moore of Orinda, California. They were members of the East Bay Rods club. The body was channeled over the frame and painted Metalflake blue. The pickup bed has been shortened, and the entire front end was chromed. A four-carb manifold neatly dresses up the 265-ci Chevy V-8. Interior features pearl white pleated upholstery with black rugs.

with *Ala Kart*, *Twister T* was powered by a hemi-head DeSoto engine. The Model T roadster had quad headlights—by now a Barris trademark—and a dazzling Metalflake Peacock Green lacquer paint job. The ante had been upped one more time, and once again all bets were off for a home-built hot rod to win the AMBR in coming years.

Indeed, a review of the subsequent AMBR winners during the 1960s clearly illustrates that home-built hot rods no longer qualified as favorites for winning America's most prestigious roadster award. The seven successive winners after *Twister T* were: Tex Smith's *XR-6* (1963), a *Hot Rod* magazine project car that was *supposed* to be an exercise in utilizing traditional hot rod building techniques, but mushroomed into a project of dynamic proportions that included the assistance of such customizers as Barris (yet another AMBR anointed with his golden touch) and Gene Winfield, to name a few; Don Tognotti's (1964) *King T*, a full-custom Model T that had a chromed Jaguar rear end, luscious lavender pearl paint job applied by Winfield, and plush white-pearl Naugahyde upholstery;

From 1963, here's *Lil Nugget*, entered by Dave Robertson of Hollydale, California. This '56 Ford custom pickup had a 390-ci '59 Cadillac engine with dual-quad carbs linked to an Eldorado transmission. Chromed spoke wheels were from a Buick Skylark. The rolled front pan meets the angled fenders, forming a grille cavity with angled Chevy quad lights and '58 Ford perforated mesh. Paint was lime gold Metalflake, and Ed Martinez did the pearl white and goldtone Naugahyde. Can you imagine this sale price of $2,350?

They were listed in the program as "Special Exhibits," but they were always a part of the Oakland Roadster Show. This example is a 1951 Harley-Davidson 74 motorcycle, belonging to Robert Cozzette of San Lorenzo, California. The bike was custom built with a 21-inch BSA front wheel, and 18-inch rear wheel. the frame has 4-inch extended fork legs, and the paint is Metalflake blue. The fuel tank was customized with metal sculpturing, matched to a Bates competition seat. The rear fender was custom, and has passenger support.

Carl Casper's (1965) wild, hand-built roadster dubbed *Casper's Ghost*; Don Lokey's (1966; and yet another rodder from Fresno who called on Barris to build a winner!) highly modified 1927 Ford pickup truck that featured old-time cowl lamps matched with a modern, sleek, hand-formed wing-shaped grille shell; Bob Reisner's (1967 and 1968) *Invader*, a from-the-ground-up roadster that utilized *two* Pontiac V-8 engines, sitting side by side, for power (and, yes, Reisner drove the car!); and finally metalsmith Joe Wilhelm's (1969) *Wild Dream* that had a hand-formed aluminum body to resemble a modified Ford Model T.

While these AMBR winners, plus countless other rods and customs, were helping alter the face of America's most prestigious car show, the human side of the equation was playing its part to make history, too. Ironically, in 1960 when presidential candidate John F. Kennedy was formulating his ideas for the New Frontier, Al Slonaker was laying the foundation for a Hall of Fame that would celebrate the forefathers of the Grand National Roadster Show. As he stated in the souvenir program that year:

In 1964, Don Tognotti of Sacramento, California, won the title of AMBR with his *King T* 1914 roadster, the oldest model to win the title. Tognotti started building in 1962 and finished in 1964. *King T's* front end featured a hand-formed tube axle, '51 Chevy coil springs, spindles, Monroe shocks, and Airheart Disc brakes. The engine was from a '55 Chevy, and used a Powerglide automatic transmission. The bodywork and pearl Chameleon paint were sprayed by Gene Winfield. Today, Tognotti produces the Oakland Roadster Show.

If you lived in Vacaville, California, and had the name of "Cruces," everybody knew who you were because of your fine workmanship in the tall T coupe that you built. Black in color, with white Naugahyde interior and black rugs, the car was typical for its time. Joe chose a 301-ci '60 Chevy with Algon fuel injectors for power. This Model T body remained stock in height but the car rode on a dropped front axle. Its unique chromed exhaust system routed forward, then back around between the rear springs and fenders. This picture is vintage 1964.

"This year the Hall of Fame is new, and outstanding pioneers in the creative car building sport have been elected for honors."

And so, with less fanfare than you'd expect, the Hall of Fame was established, commemorated by a single ceremony on Sunday evening, February 21, 1960, to announce and introduce the charter members. Fittingly, Slonaker was among the inductees chosen for this honor roll. He was joined by Joe Bailon, George Barris, Mrs. Harold Casaurang, Ezra Ehrnhardt, Romeo Palamides, Wally Parks, Robert E. Petersen, Gordon Vann, and Walt Woron. Ironically, Mary Slonaker wasn't included as a charter member, although that oversight would be rectified in 1962.

Almost immediately the Hall of Fame became an integral part of the annual Roadster Show, with ceremonies to welcome new inductees held sometime during the first few days of each show. During the Hall of Fame's first seven years—1960–1966—the inductee list eventually swelled to 64 members. Then, curiously before the 1967 show, the promoters suspended the Hall of Fame from the show's agenda, and this prestigious gathering of eagles was allowed to wither on the vine. It was, however, reinstated in 1988, but during its 21-year hiatus the Hall of Fame remained packed away, hidden from sight.

The AMBR and Hall of Fame weren't the only causes for celebration in 1960. As the show entered its second decade, the number of awards handed out to participants reached 68. At stake were 20 National Class Championship awards, plus a like number of U.S. Western Class Championship and California State Championship awards that car builders vied for.

But the big plums remained the Grand National Sweepstakes awards with the AMBR trophy serving as the crown jewel. Along with the AMBR award were: Semi Custom Car d'Elegance, Full Custom Car d'Elegance, America's Best Competition Car (which shared rights to the perpetual AMBR trophy with the top roadster winner), America's Best Sports Car, America's Best Hot Rod, The People's Choice, and the Car Contributing Most to Automotive Progress.

By now competition among the show car exhibitors for these awards had become fierce, and to counter some of the bitterness felt among nonwinners, the following notice—written with a hint of sarcasm, no doubt—was printed in the 1961 program:

"Judging any contest is a ticklish endeavor. In the National Roadster Show it is one of the toughest tasks the experts have ever faced. Winners, of course, think the judges do a fine job. But losers often would like to poke some of the judges in the nose. So, to protect noses, the Show doesn't publicize the judges. To give visitors some idea of how experts rate the amazing cars here, the Show presents an excerpt from the judging charts."

The program then listed a brief description of how the judges tabulated the points. There were five categories to be judged, worth a maximum of 20 points each. The categories included: Show Appeal (the judges looked for showmanship of the car's display, eye appeal of the craftsmanship, etc.), Safety (essentially to evaluate the roadworthiness of the vehicle to make sure that it was safe to drive!), Condition (overall appearance of the car's paint, engine compartment, interior, etc.), Workmanship (examining the alignment of body parts and seams, smoothness of the panels' surfaces, undercarriage finish, etc.), and Innovations (selection of parts, incorporation of unusual designs, new ideas, etc.). Using this list, a judge evaluated a car, in the process putting at risk life, limb—and nose!

Winning—and losing—awards wasn't the only incentive for entering the National Roadster Show. In an

Even young kids had a place at the Oakland Show. In 1964, Jim Stewart of Hayward, California, displayed his flamed quarter-midget racer. The front axle, front and rear nerf bars, and roll over bar were completely chromed. Red Lee of Oakland did the blue Metalflake paint job with a dark blue flame pattern and gold pinstriped edges. Pleated black Naugahyde covered the bucket seat.

Another member of the East Bay Rods display was George Young's '27 T Ford roadster pickup. The front end, springs, wishbones, and quick-change rear end are completely chromed. Nestled inside the black lacquer frame was a 350-ci Oldsmobile with outside type headers. The body was painted white with contrasting purple panel scallops and light purple pinstripes. The interior was finished with black pleated Naugahyde and a matching tonneau cover over the cab and on the pickup bed.

In the semi-custom hardtop class at the 1964 show was South San Francisco's Paul Yeager and his '55 Chevy hardtop. Painted metallic green, with Tommy the Greek-accented light green scallops, teardrops and white pinstriping, the Chevy was dressed with Corvette grille bars set in the stock grille opening. Under the hood huffed a 327-ci fuel injected engine with a four-speed transmission spinning 4.56 Positraction rear gears. Popular then, as now, were American mag wheels.

effort to expand the scope of the Oakland show, custom auto makers were encouraged to build one-off cars other than what were construed as hot rods and customs. These offshoots addressed several design topics, including experimental, or futuristic, and alternative-energy autos.

As early as 1960 the show's promoters posted a $5,000 incentive reward "to the first person (or group) to develop a functional solar steam-powered hot rod, sport car or custom car." The primary stipulation to collect the award was that the vehicle had to be unveiled at the Oakland show.

Stated the promoters, "In this manner, we of the National Roadster Show hope in some measure to speed research and development in this field so that creative car builders will do some serious work in solar steam science, engineering and mechanics." Fittingly, the show's theme for 1960 was "Glorifying American Ingenuity in Automotive Progress."

Nobody ever collected the $5,000 bounty, but the fol-

lowing year the Roadster Show became the showcase for several interesting futuristic designs. It was a portent of things to come at Oakland, especially for the immediate years, as car builders began to show a stronger willingness to try new and imaginative designs, even when it came to creating candidates for America's Most Beautiful Roadster.

Among the early exotics, or experimental, cars were the *XPAK 400* and *X-61*, built by George Barris and Andrew DiDia, respectively. Barris fans remember the *XPAK 400* as an early attempt at creating a car that would never experience a flat tire. That's because the *XPAK 400* rode on a cushion of air, and had no wheels or tires. The car, sponsored by *Car Craft* magazine, was elevated 5 inches above the ground, thanks to a series of 20-inch cast aluminum fans positioned on the vehicle's belly pan. The fans pointed downward to blow air that would raise the car above the road surface. The 422-pound vehicle was propelled forward by a revolving jet nozzle, so that the thrust

My last entry for 1964 is this '31 Ford roadster owned by Jim Miraglia of San Leandro, California. In the engine compartment was a 389-ci Pontiac equipped with a GMC cam and three-carb Edelbrock manifold. Whitewall tires dressed the slotted Astro chrome wheels. Paint was Matador Red with Tommy the Greek black and white pinstriping. The black Naugahyde upholstery was a product of Glen's Custom upholstery.

could be pointed in different directions to steer the vehicle. The *XPAK* held one person, and resembled a small space craft with a pair of stabilizer fins on either side. The total length for the *XPAK 400* was 12 feet, measuring 6 feet wide and 30 inches high. The aluminum and plastic body was painted pearl lacquer. To underscore the importance of the *XPAK 400*, *Motor Trend* magazine, one of *Car Craft's* sister publications within the Petersen Publishing family, proclaimed Barris' air car "the most valuable contribution to the automotive industry of the year," as stated in the 1961 show program.

The *X-61* wasn't as radical. In fact, even with its ungainly tail fins, protruding rear deck, and massive rear bubble window, the *X-61* looked much like a Cadillac that the General Motors-owned company might have produced had their styling department been headed by the likes of West Coast customizers Joe Bailon, Joe Wilhelm, or Gene Winfield.

In reality, the *X-61* was created by Andrew DiDia, of Detroit, Michigan, and completed by ClarKaiser Custom Shop. DiDia described the *X-61* as a "dream car," which meant that it had features that he projected

Jim Mack, from Fremont, California, owned this '26 T touring. Powered by a 283-ci Corvette engine with a Duntov cam and dual carbs, the tub had chrome outside headers built by Mack that were routed into Porter mufflers. The drivetrain was a mix-match of early and late Ford ware: a '39 Ford transmission with a late-model rear end. The black rolled-and-pleated Naugahyde upholstery looks good with the orange lacquer paint. Big and little tires were mounted on classy Chrysler wire wheels.

For 1965, the AMBR trophy went to Carl Casper of Mount Morris, Michigan, for his wild hand-built fiberglass body roadster known as *Casper's Ghost*. There was nothing ghostly about its powerplant, though. The *Ghost* had a 426 -ci Pontiac V-8 that was fed by a pair of 4-71 GMC Superchargers. Toss in pearl white paint with candy red frosting overtones, white and red Naugahyde upholstery and top, and you had one AMBR winner. Interestingly, AMBR candidates didn't loose points for not running back then.

would one day be adopted by mainstream automakers for their consumer cars. DiDia scored a few bull's-eyes in future-think, too, with the *X-61*. Direct hits by DiDia included disappearing windshield wipers and headlights, and red lights on the doors that automatically turned on when the doors were opened to warn of oncoming traffic—options and features found on many cars built today. As for the *X-61* itself, its future lay with the pop singer Bobby Darrin, who bought it from DiDia.

Not to be outdone at the 1961 show, one hard-core customizer, above all others, showed up with a rather flashy custom of his own creation. Bill Cushenbery, working from his shop in nearby Monterey, California, returned to Oakland with his altered 1940 Ford coupe for 1961. The editors of *Hot Rod* wrote—in the typical abbreviated, chop-chop verbiage found in Petersen Publishing captions of that era—in their show report: "Sensation of the Oakland show was Bill Cushenberry's [sic] revamped '40 Ford coupe, one of the most interesting customs with a hot rod flair. It goes beyond the usual chop and section (4 1/2 and 5 inches) with

abbreviation of lower area normally occupied by running boards, using bottom lip to accent formed fender scoops. Grille is of perforated metal, oval tube, foreign lights."

In two accompanying photo captions, *Hot Rod*'s description of Cushenbery's '40 reveals even more about building methods and custom design techniques of the era. States one caption: "Coupe's interior is, possibly, wilder than the exterior. Plush padding, bucket seats and headrests are evident here but we'll have to wait for further photo coverage to fully appreciate this builder's novel treatment of the dash panel and abbreviated steering wheel. Look closely and you will notice that the instruments are encased in a center console between the seats. Car is painted Pearlescent Red, dubbed 'El Matador' by owner."

Cushenbery's coupe was, by all means, one of the highlights of the show. Concluded *Hot Rod* in its show report about *El Matador*: "Wide stance, done by offsetting wheel rims, enhances lowness of coupe, as do extended and tunneled headlight openings. Wheel beautification is realized by chrome plating and substitution of center spinner

My last shot from 1965 is this '32 Ford pickup truck from Orinda, California. Owner Mike Clausen had the top chopped and the bed shortened. Notice the chrome exhaust pipes running up and alongside the bed, a popular 1950s style. Under the hood was a polished aluminum firewall showing off the '50 Olds engine with three carbs. The interior was trimmed with white Naugahyde.

flanked by furniture drawer knobs. Note stock Ford two-piece windshield has been replaced with a single-piece glass, adding much to the smooth appearance of the coupe. Even tires, U.S. Royal Masters, were specially selected for the fine design of their sidewalls."

The show report included photos of several other interesting cars, among them John Snyder's '27 Ford roadster pick-up. The caption concluded, "Roadsters were still in abundance," as if to reassure the reader that the National Roadster Show was, indeed, supposed to be about hot rod roadsters. Even so, the story lacked a photograph of Guasco's AMBR-

winning '29. Instead, the only mention of America's Most Beautiful Roadster appeared buried in a caption that talked about car owners at the show putting last-minute touches to their cars before the judges made their rounds. Concluded the caption: "Dick Guasco's street roadster won 'Most Beautiful' title."

Ironically, all the hubbub given to the wild and radical show cars may have spawned the formation of a new word in hot rodding's vernacular, for as near as can be determined the phrase "street rod" first appeared in the Oakland Roadster Show report in the July 1962 issue of *Rod & Custom*. In the

Feature Cars
Freaks or Fantasy?

No doubt the nine-foot-tall America's Most Beautiful Roadster trophy commands center stage at the Grand National Roadster Show. Fittingly, the Goliath-sized trophy has been the main attraction since the show's inception in 1950, representing the pinnacle of showmanship among hot rodders in America, if not the world.

But the AMBR trophy and the hot rod roadsters that compete for it aren't the only major attractions that draw people to Oakland for the Granddaddy of all car shows. The spectators, who pay good money to pass through the turnstiles, also come to see what the show promoters term as "feature cars."

As you might expect, the event's feature cars don't necessarily compete for awards and trophies. Instead, these special attractions are actually invited—sometimes paid, because oftentimes the promoters offer the car owners appearance money for their participation—to attend, serving as sideshow novelties for the crowd to view and enjoy.

Feature cars aren't unique to the Roadster Show, but Oakland was among the first custom car shows to capitalize on them. Indeed, as early as the second National Roadster Show in 1951, promoters Al and Mary Slonaker realized the money value that non-competing cars and exhibits offered the show.

One of the first sideshows was the build-up of a hot rod roadster that took place inside the Exposition Building during the 1951 six-day show (February 20–25). The work was performed by, in the words of the show's official souvenir program, "Bay Area mechanics and speed racing men." In addition, two jet aircraft engines—novelties for the time—were displayed by the U.S. Navy. For the record, the engines included a J33 and J35. Both engines "burn high-grade kerosene," according to the program's write-up.

The aerial theme maintained its flight of fantasy into the following year, this time with an exhibit showcasing the world's first flying automobile (a novelty then, and now!). The Third Annual souvenir program read, in part:

In the air, the flying automobile has a top speed over 110 miles per hour and cruising speed over 100 miles per hour. Rate of climb is in excess of 500 feet per minute; the craft has a service ceiling of 12,000 feet and a cruising range over 300 miles. It lands at 50 miles per hour within 300 feet and needs 655 feet to take off. Fuel

consumption, cruising, is eight gallons per hour. It requires four minutes to change from plane to car.

The next year, February 17–22, 1953, the show featured one of the few 1948 Tucker cars ever made. The program mentioned that the short-lived Tucker auto company had been embroiled in controversy from the beginning, making it "one of the biggest news stories in the automobile world." Ironically, the program also pointed out that the Tucker was included in the show "because we believe the public is vitally interested in any automobile, whether it be 'the car of the future' or merely an impractical freak."

Feature cars remained an integral part of the show, reaching a zenith in the mid-1960s when they began sharing equal billing with the show cars themselves. Perhaps the high point was at the February 12–22, 1965, show when the *Munster Koach* that George Barris built for the *Munsters* television series was featured on the program's cover. Two years later (February 17–26, 1967), the famed *Batmobile* appeared on the program's cover. And—holy crowd!—you realize just how big a draw *Batmobile* was when, even though the show's souvenir program included only a brief two-column-inch story about it inside, spectators queued in lines that stretched endlessly down the show's aisles so that they could enjoy a closer look at one of Hollywood's biggest attractions.

Other sideshow celebrities of the 1960s included such unique cars as the *Surf Woody* and *Turbo-Sonic* (also Barris creations), Romeo Palamides' jet-powered dragster (good for 259 miles per hour in the quarter mile; he also had plans to build a rocket-powered car with intentions of breaking the sound barrier on land), Les Weber's *Shark*, and the sleek bubble-topped *Manta Ray* that Dean Jeffries crafted based on his experiences at the Indianapolis 500.

Even though the feature cars were—and continue to be—major hits at Oakland (and other car shows throughout the country), in all probability these "freaks" wouldn't maintain their spectator appeal if it weren't for the real stars of the show. And those stars continue to be the cars that compete for all the class awards and trophies, among them the nine-foot loving cup that can go to only one car in the country—America's Most Beautiful Roadster.

brief story that lacked a byline, the author wrote, "Other popular items that were much used on the street rods were polished mag, wire and chromed wheels . . ."

Even so, the skimpy one-line mention of Guasco's AMBR car was like a subliminal message to entries for 1962. And the message was that it was time for a change, time to get radical. The free spirit of the sixties was about to uncork itself on Oakland.

The precursor to this was another experimental car known as *X-1970 Vortex*, built by Jerry Woodward of Provo, Utah. *X-1970* appeared on the 1962 show's program cover, and was billed as "the first 1970 automobile." People viewed *Vortex* so ahead of its time that, stated the show program's feature story of the car, "it has been renumbered the X-2000, for experts believe it shows a glimpse of design for automobiles of the next century."

Perhaps *X-1970*'s (or X-2000, if you will) most realistic future-think was its front suspension that was designed to adapt to "radar roads." Moreover, Woodward's radar-friendly concept was recently put into effect for several California roads in 1997, so the three-wheeler, it turns out, maintained a direct link to the future, and actually beat the year-2000 deadline. *Vortex* also served up a few other amenities found in today's cars: the passenger door locked from the driver's side, and thermostatically-controlled electric fans helped draw cool air to the radiator.

About the time that some designers were tampering with the future, using experimental cars to do their talking, the editors at *Rod & Custom* decided it was time to focus on two of the custom world's hard-core builders—George Barris and Ed "Big Daddy" Roth. A classic interview was conducted with these two stylists that appeared as a two-part story shared by the May and June 1962 issues. The two-in-one interview gave some interesting insight about these men, considered among the most imaginative and enterprising builders of their time. Their comments reflected many of the trends and attitudes found at Oakland, too.

Bill Neumann, editor of *Rod & Custom* in 1962, conducted the interview. He explored some interesting issues, among them the fact that Barris represented the established order of hand-formed metal working, while Roth was exploring the new frontier offered by fiberglass. The following excerpts from the interview's Part 1 give valuable insight as to how Barris and Roth approached their respective goals:

Neumann: "George, is metalwork just as expensive as building a glass body?"

Barris: "Metal is more expensive. You've got more handwork, and you've got to have craftsmen. We're from the old school, where you have to build forms and you form the metal around it, seam it together with either lap-joints and bend-joints, hammer-weld it out and then lead in the seams. I've always been this way, and I feel this is probably the best way to do it, but it is much more expensive. Your top metal

Oakland Show, 1966: Norman Hopkins of Fresno named his '29 Ford pickup *Woodell*. Under the hood rested a 283-ci '58 Chevy V-8 linked to a '39 Ford transmission modified to an open driveline '48 Ford rear end. The Riverside red and brown tuck-and-roll Naugahyde combination is proof that the high-tech rodders didn't invent that combo. Tree huggers will appreciate the headliner—made of wood—and the ash-panel camper shell.

craftsmen are making pretty good money."

Neumann: "Do you feel that way, Ed?"

Roth: "Metal is definitely more expensive. That's why everybody that plans to build a car for the show circuit or for show will have to consider fiberglass—because unless they're really loaded, they won't have a chance to have a way-out custom. With fiberglass they have at least a decent chance to sculpture, as George says, their own design. The sculptured look is one that is definitely coming, which means—sculpting means that it's more a unit custom than a bolt-on custom—you know, little fins here, little fins there. And since the sculptured look was started here on the West Coast, and is gradually going East due to the interchange of car shows, and guys traveling east, I think that gradually if anybody's going to consider a wild sculptured custom, fiberglass will be the answer for it."

In Part 2 of the June 1962 issue, Neumann touched on the subject of the custom car crowd's influence on Detroit's auto stylists. Barris' and Roth's comments were a sign of things to come, both in Detroit and the custom car show scene:

Sure looks like an old-style hot rod! This '27 roadster on Deuce rails belonged to Robert Skibo of Lodi, California. The engine was a '47 Mercury flathead with high compression heads and three-carb manifold. The front end was chromed, and check out the radius rod brackets. The medium blue lacquer gave the spectator a choice other than black!

Stated Barris: ". . . I recently sat in a meeting with the top stylists of GM and Ford, and they have definitely told me that many of the cars I've built did influence them."

Added Roth: ". . . We'll have to stay ahead of Detroit, that's for certain, so to stay ahead of Detroit we'll have to do so way-out in our thinking and styling that it'll just be unbelievable to imagine what'll be seen in a car show of, say, 10 years from now."

And so opened the door for even more wild and crazy designs for customs, experimentals, even hot rods. The trip through the 1960s was going to be wilder yet. Again, we can turn to the pages of *Rod & Custom* for evidence. The July 1966 issue included that year's Oakland show coverage. The concluding photo caption for a trio of wild show cars read:

"Here are three examples of something that was completely unknown 16 years ago . . . the out-and-out show car. Designed and built from scratch, these cars are 'idea' or 'novelty' items, for use only in car shows. It's safe to say that the philosophy has changed since the old days. Car shows used to be something that would give the public a chance

Another 1966 entry is Curtis Conner's '23 T roadster pickup, from Elk Grove, California. Named *Golden Bucket*, it has a 96-inch wheelbase with a boxed tube frame. The pickup rode on a chromed four-inch dropped axle, with power supplied by a '58 Chevy V-8, four-speed Pontiac hydro transmission, and a '40 Ford rear end with quick change. The paint was gold Metalflake; the interior pearl white Naugahyde.

America's Most Beautiful Roadster for 1967 was Bob Reisner's *Invader* . The body was hand-formed from aluminum, and Reisner spared nothing on the powertrain, doubling up on everything—the drivetrain includes *two* Pontiac GTO engines, *two* hydro transmissions, and *two* Jaguar rear ends. The car has independent suspension at all four corners, and the custom body was finished with pearl-white and candy red paint by Joe Anderson. The red velvet interior was the product of Joe Perez's needle and thread.

From Los Gatos, California, Steve Lawson entered his '32 Ford high-boy roadster in the '67 show. The root-beer-brown metallic contrasted well with the white Naugahyde upholstery by Warren Thatcher of San Mateo, California. Under the hood sat a 296-ci '48 Mercury flathead, with a four-inch stroke, Harmon & Collins Super T cam, four Stromberg 97 carbs, and Offenhauser high compression heads. The front end, headers, and undercarriage were all chromed.

to see what the rodders were doing, and the kind of cars that were being built. Now the cars are built to entertain the public, and are contracted for, like performers."

Among those contracted performers were a few cars that starred in television and Hollywood movies. Cars such as the *Monkeemobile*, *Munster Koach* and *Surf Woody* became marquee hits at car shows across the country, including the Grand National Roadster Show in Oakland.

But perhaps the biggest celebrity car was the *Batmobile*, built by—you guessed it—George Barris for the *Batman* television series that was syndicated by ABC Television Network in 1966. Barris said that he and his crew (including the likes of noted fabricators and customizers Dick Dean and Dean Jefferies) built the *Batmobile* for the television series in three weeks. The famed *Batmobile* was loaded with "Bat" goodies, and was a smash hit among the car show crowd in 1966 and 1967 when the television show enjoyed its zenith among viewers. Harold "Baggy" Bagdasarian, who promoted the nearby Sacramento Autorama and who would one day purchase the Oakland show from the Slonakers, said that the *Batmobile* was the biggest draw ever for him as a promoter. When Baggy displayed the *Batmobile* on the show floor at Sacramento, spectators waiting to see it up close formed

The hot rodder's choice, a '32 Ford roadster! Many were at Oakland in 1967, and this one belonged to Bob Cerelli. This Deuce was typical for its time, riding on a dropped axle with tube shocks, and shoed with '40 Ford hydraulic brakes all around. The engine was Corvette with dual carbs, and the interior had black Naugahyde custom-built bucket seats. The running boards were covered and padded in Naugahyde, a trend that was dying out by 1967. The paint was Light Apple Green Metallic.

Once again, the kids are involved in Oakland. Here's Shannon Criss of Castro Valley, California, with his customized quarter midget, named *Shamrock II*. The engine is air cooled, with the racer sports gold alloy wheels, black Naugahyde upholstery and a brilliant Candy Red paint job with slim blue scallops and white striping. Criss was the 1966 Grand National Champion.

lines that wound throughout the show, blocking other car displays and vendor booths. Barris charged $3,000 appearance money for the *Batmobile*. Cited Baggy, "It more than doubled that at the gate."

The nine-foot AMBR trophy was bumped farther from center stage during the 1960s when the show promoters initiated another award, called the Tournament of Fame, an invitational class that was billed as "over and above all regular competition in The Show."

Essentially, the Tournament of Fame was for professional car builders. As the show program explained, "for creative car builders who have won a place in the sun as exhibitors in the Roadster Show and who are now famous as professionals with their own shops."

To be sure, the Tournament entrants for 1962 included some heavy hitters from Oakland's past. Among the list were Joe Bailon, George Barris, Bill Cushenbery, Darryl Starbird, and Joe Wilhelm. Their entries were: *El Tangerino* (Bailon's custom that was billed with "many features not seen on custom cars"); *Astra* (Barris' magnesium-bodied coupe costing an astounding $15,000 to build in 1961); *Silhouette* (Cushenbery's bubble-topped speedster formed from 20-gauge sheet metal); *Futurista* (Starbird's three-wheel dream car); and *Wild Dream* (Wilhelm's aluminum-body roadster). The winner was awarded a trip for two to the Paris Auto Show later that year. And the winner was— Bill Cushenbery and *Silhouette*!

Practically lost in the hubbub of that first Tournament of Fame was the presentation of the nine-footer to LeRoi "Tex" Smith's *XR-6* and Bob Tindle's '32 Sedan *Orange*

Crate. Wait a minute, *two* winners, and one isn't even a roadster? Well, yeah, see, for a few years—1957 through 1971 to be exact—the perpetual AMBR trophy was shared by the most beautiful roadster (naturally) and what the promoters termed America's Best Competition Car. In fact, during the years that the trophy was shared by these two class winners, the roadster winner was also referred to as America's Best Roadster.

Another change took place during the 1960s that had a profound effect on Oakland: the 1950s-style custom car, whose popularity was fading like a cheap paint job in the sun, was in decline among builders. For years customizers had relied on their savvy in the junkyard to create these flashy-looking cars. By mix-matching parts that they pirated from junked cars, customizers created some interesting rides—for the street and for the show. Of course, the pro customizers, who built many cars specifically for show purposes, relied on their metal-forming talents to chop, channel, and smooth bodies to create dazzling one-of-a-kind show cars. Lost in the whimsical times of the 1960s, though, was the art of customizing a car by selecting and sizing castaway parts from other cars. This parts matching had been an integral part of the American custom car scene throughout the previous decade. Now it was losing its luster.

Indeed, by the mid-1960s America's car culture was steadily steering in the opposite direction from customs. Even hot rods, a style of car spawned by the jalopy movement of early post-World War II years, was staring change in the face. Waiting in the wings was what came to be termed "muscle cars," instant hot rods built and sold by Detroit's auto manufacturers. As early as 1963 the writing was on the wall, as evidenced by the storied interview that *Rod & Custom* conducted in its July 1963 issue with seven of the leading customizers of the time. Among those interviewed were Barris, Starbird, Winfield, and Cushenbery, who represented Ford's Custom Car Caravan and AMT Custom Consultant Team; Ed Roth, who was contracted to Revell Models; Starbird, who was similarly hired by Monogram; and Wilhelm.

At one point in the interview Starbird stated, "Let's face it, the custom cars are slowly dying. I mean the old-type custom car where we did the headlights, taillights, chopped the top, and this type thing. They're almost dead as you can see right here in this Oakland show."

Starbird, and the others, agreed that the next generation custom car would come from Detroit, although the consensus, too, was that it was up to the creative genius of the pro builders to lead the way to new and exciting concepts. Among those concepts were what Winfield termed "more emphasis on futuristic cars and the experimental cars, both roadsters and bubble top arrangements."

Offered Cushenbery, "I am working on what I think might be something different. It has off-center styling, sort

of abstract I think. We are going to try it out. I personally think it might go over pretty well. I don't really know . . . certainly have to give it a whirl." Of course, Cushenbery was talking about the asymmetrical look that came into vogue about that time, and was even adopted by Detroit's leading car makers of the time.

Perhaps the true colors—and a sign of those wild times—was presented by Big Daddy himself, Ed Roth. The *Rod & Custom* interview concluded with Roth, who posed the following regarding his new threads, a tuxedo and top hat (which were to become trademark attire):

Well, I was painting shirts at the Oakland show and I heard a fellow standing in back of me mumbling something about the bunch of nasty hot rodders being beatnics [sic]. So I figured, what can we do? . . . Now I am on a personal crusade to clean up the hot rod field. I would like everybody to take a bath and put on a necktie at the car shows, and it is not very painful to take a bath and put on a tie because I did it for the Oakland show especially and I am going to contin-

ue to do it, so that your fathers can respect you and they will give you more money for gas to drive around the town and they will give you more money to spend on your car. It really works, because my wife gave me a little more money to spend at the Oakland show just because I took a bath.

Roth's statement, although heavily accented with Big Daddy's typical wit and sarcasm, truly raises another interesting point: By the mid-1960s the Grand National Roadster Show helped comprise a network of custom car shows that stretched across the country. The West Coast, especially, was home to many legendary shows, among them the Sacramento Autorama, Seattle Autorama, Monterey Kar Kapades, and Los Angeles Winternationals Auto Show. On the East Coast the Hartford Autorama was king, joined by many other events that capitalized on the hot rod and custom car movement east of the Mississippi River. The popularity of these custom car shows formed the foundation for a cottage industry that, even today, services the owners and builders of show cars and street-driven customs throughout the country. Indeed, Barris has, on more than one occasion, publicly stated that car shows such as Oakland helped create an auto aftermarket industry that today accounts for billions of dollars spent in our nation's economy. Specifically, Barris points out that chrome shops, paint shops, body shops, trim shops, even bolt-on accessory makers owe a large part of their existence to the car show scene.

At the '67 show, Doug Stroming's '58 Chevy Impala was really gorgeous! The side scoops in back of the door were frenched, the side trim was reversed by putting rear fender trim on the front fender, and the fender wells were of stainless steel. The custom grille insert was from a Corvette. A 370-ci engine was backed by a four-speed transmission. The Naugahyde interior matches the Jade Pearl and Candy Green Mist paint job.

In 1968, Bob Reisner's *Invader* and Joe Wilhelm's *Wild Dream* custom hand-formed aluminum-bodied roadster tied for AMBR. The *Wild Dream's* engine and transmission were from a Chevy, while the rear end was based on a modified Mercury third member. This three-quarter rear view shows the extensive fin work and Metalflake gold paint edged in tangerine. Coming in through the rear door wearing the red shirt is the legendary Petersen Publishing Co. ace photographer, my hero and friend for many years, Eric Rickman.

This burgeoning aftermarket business serves as a double-edged sword, however. For as the industry grows, it becomes more commercialized, and much of the personalized, down-home flavor that was a part of the National Roadster Show in the 1950s was lost by the end of the 1960s. Perhaps customizer Joe Bailon's words sum it up best, "From '51 through the mid-sixties were the best times of our lives. It was nothing but fun. Life was different then. You could take five dollars and have a good dinner. Those were the good years. You didn't have that big worry over you. Money doesn't go very far no more."

The 1960s. They were the best of times; they were the worst of times. Adds Bailon about his part in the play known as Oakland, "Although the money wasn't there (for building customs), your work was appreciated."

As the decade of flower power, free love, and free thinking reached its zenith, it managed to smother the innocence of a bygone era. With the 1970s approaching, Oakland, as did the rest of America, geared up for some truly psychedelic times.

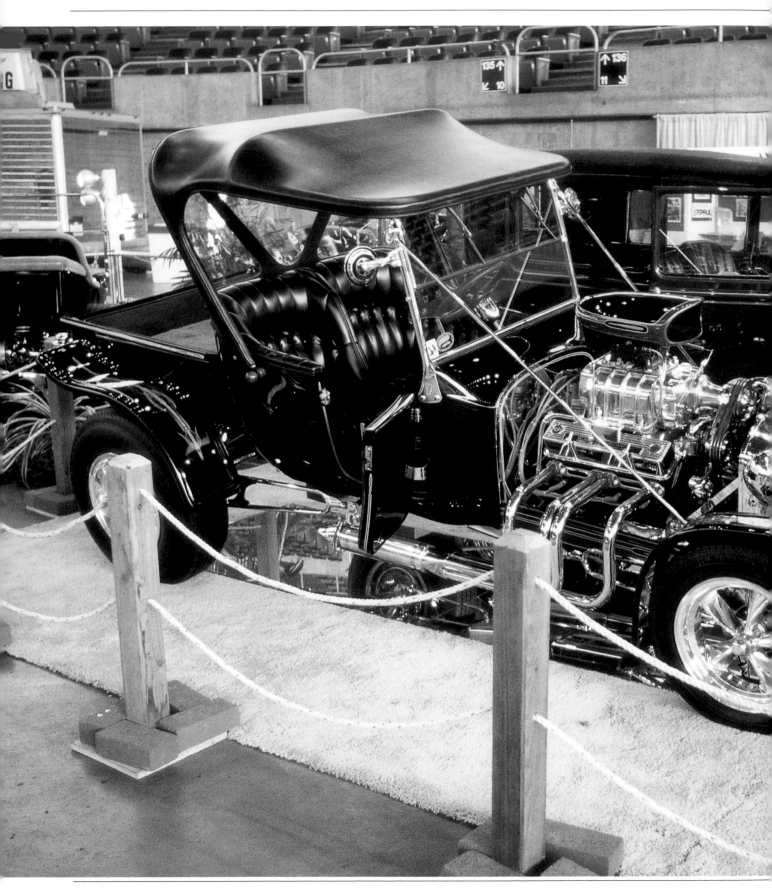

1970–1979
The Psychedelic Years

Prior to 1970 Andy Brizio was essentially known within the Roadster Show's social circle for the T-shirts and decals that he hawked from his booth at local car shows and his shop in South San Francisco, California. Yet over the years Brizio, had been an integral part of the Oakland Roadster Show, sometimes helping prepare the show hall for the forthcoming event, sometimes helping clean up after the last car left. He also had entered several cars in show competition at Oakland, and in 1968 he even promoted his new *Instant T* kit car by assembling a complete car on the exhibit floor during that year's 10-day show.

Despite these flirtings in show car competition, nobody truly expected Brizio to ever win rights to the nine-foot trophy, because he was considered a T-shirt guy or the fellow you visited when you needed decals for your car. He was, essentially, an entrepreneur with a knack for turning a profit—make that an instant profit, thanks to the success he enjoyed with the *Instant T*. But an AMBR winner? Hardly. Based on the rites of passage that had been established by AMBR winners during the previous two decades, that honor was reserved for serious car builders. Certainly not for a guy who based his AMBR entry on a kit car that, for the most part, represented an ensemble of hot rod and aftermarket parts he sold as a package enabling anybody to build a similar car at home.

Even so, in 1969 Brizio decided to take the plunge and build a serious AMBR contender. Having entered his own

Ts were popular in 1979. Seen here is Dennis Imfeld's '23 Ford roadster pickup. The chassis by Roy Brizio Street Rods was fitted with Andy's tires and wheels. Cub Barnett built the blown 350-ci Chevy mill, while the body and paint were from the labors of Steve Archer. Custom pinstriping and added paint were by Mike Farley. Ken Foster was responsible for the tuck-and-rolled upholstery.

Previous Page
The 1970 AMBR winner was Andy Brizio from South San Francisco. Art Himsl painted the T's lacquer in psychedelic ribbons and scallops. Andy chose a 301-ci small-block engine from a '57 Chevy for power. And for instant results, he blessed the motor with a 4-71 GMC supercharger. Horsepower was rated at 450. The brown leather upholstery and carpets were done by Mack of Sacramento. Too numerous to mention individually, the complete undercarriage of the roadster was chromed. Later that year Andy drove his AMBR roadster to the first-ever NSRA Street Rod Nationals, held in Peoria, Illinois.

personal *Instant T* in the Grand National Roadster Show two years running, Brizio was determined that he'd get the Big Trophy, as many people called the AMBR award, in 1970. Furthermore, he would do it with his *Instant T*. It was a brilliant decision, one that not only showcased his affordable kit car, but helped cement the T-bucket roadster as the mainstay for hot rodding's trends through the remainder of the decade. In fact, there would be seven Model Ts that would win the AMBR award in the 1970s.

Brizio's AMBR plan was simple: he'd dazzle people at the Oakland Roadster Show with brilliance, by means of a flashy paint job and precision assembly detail. The man chosen to create the dazzling paint job was local custom painter *cum* artist Art Himsl. Himsl was no stranger to Oakland, either. He and his brother Mickey had won the AMBR trophy in 1969 with a custom-formed roadster boasting a fabulous paint job that was surpassed only by Brizio's 1970 entry. Himsl also was well known among the motorcycle crowd, and when the custom bike movement kicked into gear near the end of the 1960s, his spray gun

Here's another AMBR, this time for 1971. Lonnie Gilbertson of Portland, Oregon, won with his fiberglass-bodied '23 T roadster pickup. This rear three-quarter view shows the complete chromed '66 Jaguar XKE rear end. The paint was a striking Candy Apple Red, and the engine was a 327-ci '67 Chevy small-block with four Weber 48 IDA carbs. Mild panel fender painting and pinstripes accent the roadster's unique look.

Gilbert Ferreira attended the 1971 show with his '23 T Volksrod. That's a 1,600-cc Volkswagen engine mounted in the rear pickup bed. Suspension was based on a torsion bar and friction shocks linked to a 4130 chromemoly tube frame. The remainder of the chassis included a dropped tube front axle and four-spoke American mag wheels with Pirelli tires. The paint was Firemist Cinnamon lacquer, and the upholstery dark brown Naugahyde. Gil was a member of the Bay Area Roadster Club.

was for hire to also help the two-wheel show-slingers stop spectators dead in their tracks.

Brizio approached Himsl in 1969, informing him of his intentions for the next year's Oakland show. "I told Art, 'let's do something wild,'" recalls Brizio about how he laid plans for 1970 Oakland. Mind you, when you tell Himsl to "do something wild," you had better, indeed, prepare for something wild, for Himsl is proof that for every action there is a reaction. His reaction to Brizio's request was perhaps one of the most radical, flamboyant paint jobs of its time. Himsl applied no less than 27 different colors to the multiribboned paint job. In addition, no two panels on Brizio's *Instant T* shared the same graphics or colors. It was truly a remarkable display of mastering colors and graphics on a hot rod.

Regardless of the paint job's brilliance, the true glory in Brizio's car could be found in the finish and detail of its assembly. Wrote *Rod & Custom*, which featured the 1970 AMBR winner on its July, 1970, cover, "Trick paint? That's nothing new! But then, neither is brown leather upholstery, fiberglass bodies, concealed wiring, and precision welding. Where does that leave individualism? We'll tell you where, with detailing."

Don't be misled, though. Brizio's AMBR T-bucket wasn't a trailer queen, as evidenced by the 4,000-mile road trip the "Rodfather"—as he became known among his hot rod peers—and his AMBR-winning T-roadster pickup took the following summer. So, while the nine-foot trophy rested peacefully in Brizio's Bay Area hot rod shop during the summer of 1970, the car that earned that trophy was

Tom Prufer of Monte Sereno, California, built a '29 Ford roadster with all the trimmings. Under the hood sat a 289-ci Ford with a big four-barrel carb and a Joe Hunt magneto. The transmission was a C-4 linked to a XKE Jaguar rear end. The aluminum hood and side panels were made by Pete Ogden. Ken Foster of A-Action Interiors of Sacramento did the upholstery.

once again earning its keep, this time transporting its enthusiastic owner to the first NSRA (National Street Rod Association) Nationals in Peoria, Illinois. Hot rods, reasoned the Rodfather, were to be driven, as well as shown. Today he states emphatically, "I don't like the fact that they (today's AMBR winners) don't drive them. They should be driving them across to the (NSRA) Nationals."

Sadly, Brizio didn't set a precedent for subsequent AMBR winners, and it was business as usual for the AMBR clan in 1971. That year's winner was Lonnie Gilbertson's full-fendered Model T, displayed with its two right-side wheels removed to showcase the chromed chassis, and its hood folded up to highlight a highly detailed late-model V-8 engine. Years later automotive historian, hot rodder, and freelance writer Greg Sharp wrote in an article celebrating the AMBR winners from 1950–1990 for *Rod & Custom* about Gilbertson's car: ". . . it looked better as displayed than it did with wheels and hood in place."

The following year experienced an about-face to the apparent Model T movement, and John Corno's rear-

engine 1930 Ford Model A won. The car, engineered by fabricator Russ Meeks, had a flip-top body that hinged at the front, exposing the engine from the rear. The chassis featured independent suspension and a driveline based on a front-wheel-drive Oldsmobile Toronado. It was a remarkable engineering exercise, but traditionalists complained that Corno's roadster wasn't practical in terms of everyday driving appeal.

Never mind, because for the next five years the AMBR recipients had the winning formula down to a T—literally. The subsequent five winners were based on Henry Ford's fabled Model T, further exemplifying rod trends of that time that favored the old flivver. The T-based winners were: Chuck Corsello (1973; Jaguar rear end, beer keg gas tank, fuel-injected Corvette engine); Jim Vasser (1974; the first touring-body to win AMBR, based on a Brizio *Instant T* chassis); Lonnie Gilbertson again (1975; repainted by Gary Crisp, and sporting handmade front independent suspension); Bob Sbarbaro (1976; another touring T, powered by a super-

Everybody digs tourings, so here is Dave and Vicki Etheridge's '28 Ford touring that appeared at the 1971 show. It's painted two-tone with black fenders and a burgundy body. Wire wheels are chromed Buick. The front axle is three-inch dropped. Under the hood was a 292-ci Corvette with a Chevy three-speed transmission going to a Chevy rear end. The upholstery is Oxblood diamond-tufted Naugahyde.

It seemed that everybody was trying to make a statement or do things differently during the 1970s. That included hot rodders who spent the decade experimenting with mind-altering styles. Shown here is a wild '29 Ford owned by Jim and Pat Gomes of Fremont, California. Named Midnight Lace, the roadster essentially was a '70s version of a traditional A-V8 roadster. The body sat on a '32 Ford frame, and an over-bored small-block Chevy engine with three carbs was chosen for power. Like most hot rods and customs of the '70s, Midnight Lace's signature was its paint job: a wild Candy Red Metalflake with blue and purple lace. And check out the wild grille insert! Like they said back in the '70s, "cosmic."

charged V-8); and Jim Molino (1977; dubbed *Candy Man*, adorned with bright candy apple colors, a bevy of polished brass fixtures and engraved chromed parts, and pearl upholstery). Based on this string of winners, the 1970s certainly deserve the nickname "The Decade of the Seven Ts."

By 1978 the car builders once again appeared to be back on the road that led to more traditional styling. Indeed, Phil Cool played it cool with a rather refined 1932 Ford highboy roadster to cop the AMBR trophy. Surprisingly, this was only the second Deuce to win the prestigious award. Up to 1978 all winners had been either Model T or Model A Fords, with the exception of Ed Bosio's '32 in 1956. After Cool's victory, members of the Oakland fraternity indicated that perhaps this cool ride marked the return to normalcy among builders. As recently as 1993 *Hot Rod* magazine's feature editor Gray Baskerville penned an article (September 1993) in which he proclaimed the 20 top trend-setting street rods to ever appear in the magazine. Among Baskerville's picks was Cool's '32, which the "Old Dad" proclaimed helped steer the magazine's editorial philosophy back to hot rods in 1978. Wrote Baskerville:

"I personally credit Cool's colorful Deuce highboy for turning HOT ROD around. As one might remember, the magazine was still mired in van mud during the late '70s, and it needed something high, hot, and heavy to free it from the plague of those sin bins. Cool's character was every bit of that. High it was. Hot, too, thanks to the fact that it was powered by a 6-71 blown 427-inch L88 that torqued through a Muncie M-21 four-speed into a '57 Olds rear end equipped with a 3.70 Posi. As for being heavy, it was that year's America's Most Beautiful Roadster winner, too. What's more, Cool's highboy had three looks. He could do the '50s, '60s, or '70s thing by changing the roadster's wheel/tire combo, and he did so with polished Halibrands, painted steelies, and Center Lines."

Hot on the heels of Cool's hot highboy was Brian Burnett's professionally built Deuce roadster which, sadly, shot down the "return to normalcy" theory quicker than

Winner of the Hot Rod d' Elegance award at the 1972 Oakland Show was Robert Epperson's '23 T fiberglass touring that he made himself when he worked for Steve Archer's Glass Products. The engine was a 327-ci Chevy with a 4-71 GMC blower. The transmission was a '58 Powerglide feeding a '57 Chevy rear end. The paint is Vitamin C Orange with Metalflake Root Beer fender inserts.

Saddam Hussein can say Scud missile. Burnett's highboy happened to be a product of Magoo's shop near Los Angeles, and the Deuce roadster was a pro-built hot rod through and through. To be sure, the roadster's curbside appeal was that of a typical Deuce highboy, maintaining a very traditional stance. But flip up either of the hood's louvered side panels and your eyes feasted on not four but six spark plug wires per bank of cylinders. This Deuce hot rod, you see, was powered by an exotic V-12 Ferrari engine, earning the roadster its curious moniker, "Deucari." The age of normalcy had been short-lived, and once again the AMBR became the domain of pro-built cars.

Another interesting phenomenon took place about that time. The 1970s pretty much marked the demise of the tail-dragger lead sled customs that had been so popular during the 1950s. For many years the lead sleds represented the basics of hot rodding, as the cars were built from what constituted existing inventory. Simply, builders of most home-grown lead sleds utilized leftover parts that they pirated from other vehicles, or scrounged at the junkyard. These cars—called "kemps" by their owners—usually were based on 1950s model vehicles. The mix-match of parts that were bolted onto most customs became somewhat of an art among the builders, and a review of the parts manifest for a typical lead sled often read like a page from an old J. C. Whitney catalog. Here's a rundown, as it appeared in the event's program, of a custom sedan entered in the 1953 Oakland show:

Owned by Ron Gotcher of Portland, Oregon, member of the Road Angels, Inc. A Custom sedan, '51 Chevrolet. All body seams have been welded and molded. Oldsmobile rear fenders, grille from Ford and Chevrolet truck, headlights Frenched, frame chopped, electric hood, doors and deck, twin spotlights. Twenty-seven coats Royal Maroon lacquer under six coats of clear lacquer. Black leather and gray mohair upholstery. All work done by Earl's Custom Shop, Portland, Ore.

Despite the color and glamour that the customs portrayed, the romance between them and the car show crowd came to a standstill by the mid-1970s, as fewer builders cared to invest time or money into these rolling pieces of parts-art. Another contributing factor to the demise of the custom as a popular styling trend was Hollywood, for many of the top custom builders from the 1950s were eventually drafted by the major motion picture and television studios to build prop cars for movies and TV series. This left a void in the number of qualified builders available to the custom car scene. The producers in Hollywood had realized quickly that the leading custom car builders offered unique talents for building one-

Oakland 1974: Edward Lee of Fremont, California, owned this '33 Ford phaeton, which was powered by a 289-ci Ford with a four-barrel carb. The automatic transmission was linked to a Positraction rear end. Goodyear tires are mounted on chromed wire wheels. The red body and black fenders made a striking combination. The interior was done in black-pleated Naugahyde.

In 1974 the *Back to the Track* '23 T roadster belonged to Tom Prufer of Los Gatos, California. Hidden under the hood sat a feisty 160-ci Capri V-6 engine. The front sported a dropped axle and lots of chrome, while the rear end had independent suspension. The car's nose piece and metal craftsmanship were by Ron Covell. The flame paint job is credited to Rod Powell; I pinstriped the edges.

Les Owen of Campbell, California, owned this '32 Ford roadster. It had a Jaguar XKE rear end and torsion bar suspension, and a 320-ci Mustang V-8 with magneto ignition. Dunlop tires were mounted on Zenith wire wheels. Owen painted the roadster two tone green with black fenders, and Ken Foster of A-Action Auto Interiors stitched the brown Naugahyde upholstery. Once again, I applied the gold pinstriping.

off cars for motion pictures, so they enticed them with a steady stream of money and work to develop special-effects vehicles for the studios' movie productions. Customizers such as George Barris, Dick Dean, Dean Jeffries, Larry Watson, and Joe Bailon found that they could make more money building crazy-cars for the film companies than they could real-world customs for the kemp car crowd.

While the car builders were grappling with trends and styles, and weighing the benefits of which market to cater—the car show scene or Hollywood—there were changes taking place behind the scenes of the Grand National Roadster Show, too. After 23 years of ownership by Al and Mary Slonaker, the Oakland Roadster Show management was about to change hands. From 1949 through 1972, the Slonakers had been the sole proprietors of the annual event, and every year, without fail, Al and Mary produced the show. They had even enlisted the help of a dependable fellow named Mel Fernandez to manage the event during actual show hours, freeing the Slonakers to take care of the business end of America's oldest hot rod car show.

Unfortunately, over time Al Slonaker developed respiratory problems, and by the early 1970s ill health had forced him to retire from his full-time job with Oakland's school district. He and Mary moved to Scottsdale, Arizona, where the drier climate proved to be more therapeutic for his bronchial condition.

Initially, the Slonakers attempted to manage the annual Oakland show from their new Arizona home, but that proved costly and tiresome. The logical thing to do was to sell, and so the offer went out. The show could be had for a reported $150,000. Almost immediately several potential buyers contacted the Slonakers about acquiring rights to

The 1953 winner of AMBR resurfaced in the 1970s, belonging to Dick Falk of Walnut Creek, California. By then, the light blue '27 Ford roadster was repainted, although it maintained its nostalgic appeal with a '48 Merc flathead V-8 engine. Blackie Gejeian owns the roadster now.

the nation's oldest custom car show. Among them was Bob Larivee, a young, enterprising man from Michigan who one day, after forming the International Show Car Association (ISCA), would become perhaps the most powerful force in the custom car show industry. Larivee's only problem was that Al Slonaker really didn't want to sell it to him. Al's wish was that the show's ownership would remain California based. Therefore, the logical choice was an established show promoter from nearby Sacramento, California, Harold Bagdasarian, or "Baggy" to everybody who knew him.

Baggy had been a prominent fixture in the custom car scene since 1950 when he helped promote the first Sacramento Autorama. In fact, that show was the second oldest on the calendar, being junior only to the Slonakers' Roadster Show in Oakland. Baggy was a hardworking promoter, one who never let a golden opportunity slip through his fingers. In fact, as far back as 1950 he realized the potential bonanza that custom car shows offered, and it was at that time that, with the help of his fellow Thunderbolts car club members, he first staged the show that would one day become known as the Sacramento Autorama.

As Baggy explained about the Sacramento show's origins, "Two of the members (of the Thunderbolts) who had roadsters each thought they had the best roadster." Sensing a potential business venture, Baggy suggested at the next club meeting that the Thunderbolts should produce a car show open to the public to see exactly which of these two boastful members, indeed, had the best set of wheels. The show was held November 11, 1950, and, as Baggy suc-

The home of the *Big Valley T* was Fresno, California. The owner was Gary Pope, and his '23 T roadster pickup had a 350-ci '69 Chevy with six carburetors on an Edelbrock manifold. The rear end was Chevy with mag center section and disc brakes. Himsl & Haas of Concord did the white, purple, and orange paint combination, highlighted by the interior's black rolled-and-pleated Naugahyde.

Now this is a custom pickup! Steve Scott's '35 Ford pickup sat on a modified '38 pickup frame. The wheelbase was a mere 98 inches. The cab was sectioned a full 5 inches, and the nose and tail were crafted from sheet aluminum. Under the hood sat a 348-ci Chevy with a three-speed transmission. The interior was blue and white diamond-tufted Naugahyde, to match the light blue pearl lacquer.

In 1974, Bay Area Roadsters member Don Varner showed his '29 Ford roadster at Oakland. He started with a Greg Turretto space frame, chromed XKE Jaguar suspension, and a 289-ci Ford Cobra engine with a four-speed Ford transmission. The custom work included a three-piece hood with louvers and side panels, BMC Black Tulip lacquer paint, and a shortened pickup bed.

cinctly put it years later, "Neither guy won. A guy from Stockton beat 'em both."

Buoyed by that first show's success, Baggy eventually set out on his own, and the Sacramento Autorama was born. Baggy immediately showed that he had showman talents, giving his show its own, distinct name—Autorama, a name he concocted based on the General Motors Motorama car show display that was so popular during the early 1950s.

Within years the Sacramento Autorama became one of the leading car shows on the West Coast, even surpassing Oakland in the number of car entries. Baggy recalls that by 1955 "our show (Sacramento) was the largest show in the number of cars," indicating that it outweighed Oakland by about 20 entries—130 to 110.

When the Grand National Roadster Show was up for bid in 1972, Baggy couldn't resist the temptation to expand his empire of West Coast Autoramas. He quickly made an offer for Oakland, and Al promptly refused. Finally, Al said he'd sell to Baggy, but for $25,000 over the asking price! As

Baggy relates the story today, Al considered Baggy his major competitor, so if Slonaker was going to release his grip on the oldest hot rod car show in America, he'd do so only after achieving a worthy profit—at the expense of his friendly adversary!

Baggy made a counteroffer. This time he brought with him a couple investors to the bargaining table. His two partners were local car enthusiast Bill Roach and famous customizer Darryl Starbird who, like Baggy, had established his own car show empire, this one in the Midwest. The triumvirate consummated the deal with the Slonakers. Within a year Roach sold his share to Baggy and Starbird, and a new Oakland dynasty was begun.

To show their appreciation for what Al Slonaker had done for the custom car world during the previous couple decades, Baggy and company instituted the Al Slonaker

Saving the Seventies
Magazine Writers Did Their Best to Glamorize Oakland at its Darkest Time

By the 1970s, the Grand National Roadster Show appeared to be losing its luster and charm among the custom car crowd. To be sure, Oakland celebrated its 25th anniversary in 1973, so the uniqueness of the show had certainly worn off. Coupled with the addition of literally dozens of other car shows held across the country, the Grand National Roadster Show no longer was necessarily grand at all.

Even so, there was something special about Oakland that set it apart from all other car shows, even the Sacramento Autorama, which was only 10 months younger than the Roadster Show. And everybody knew that this uniqueness had to do with Oakland being the oldest hot rod show in existence. Just as nobody forgets who finished first in a race, so too the custom car crowd always remembered that Oakland was the first hot rod show to be held on an annual basis. Seniority had its privileges.

And it was Oakland's seniority and longevity that helped form the storyline for many a hot rod magazine editor's report when it came time to pen a story about the Granddaddy of all car shows. Especially during the 1970s when the show was considered just another car show among enthusiasts.

The following excerpts from some of these reports gives a better understanding today about how the automotive magazine industry regarded the Grand National Roadster Show, the Granddaddy car show of them all:

Bud Bryan for *Rod & Custom* (July 1971): "No, not the biggest in terms of total units displayed. No, not the biggest in terms of promotional grandstanding. Yes; the most talked about and greatest attended indoor show of them all. Because—at the risk of sounding provincial—this is where you'll find the best machinery, both street driven and show-*only* types.

Quality in both cases improves annually. But the change Oakland attendees notice most thrives within that street-driven contingent; they are simply cleaner than ever before. *True* automobiles, built-to-be-driven (not just into and out of shows), they often upstage without much effort supposed 'feature' vehicles."

Tex Smith for *Rod Action* (May 1973): "The Grand National Roadster Show, nee Oakland Roadster Show, may not be the largest rod and custom extravaganza in the country. It may not even get the most publicity, but year in, year out it somehow remains the most prestigous [sic] rod show in the nation. Sometimes the show is snubbed by the press, sometimes car owners decide to go elsewhere on the annual Washington's Birthday dates, sometimes the Northern California rains hold the spectators to a minimum—but always the show survives and bounces back with renewed enthusiasm."

Dick Mendonca for *Rod Action* (June 1974): ". . . No, it isn't the largest show in the country, and it doesn't draw the greatest number of participants, but it really is a kind of granddaddy . . . there is a certain amount of sophistication attached to the Oakland Roadster Show, and to win here, or even just to participate, marks the enthusiast with a kind of credential hard to achieve anywhere else. That is what has grown to be the mystique of Oakland."

Steve Coonan for *Street Rodder* (June 1978): "The Oakland Roadster Show may not be the world's biggest, best, or most prestigious custom autorama. Other car shows may have more entries, more colored lights, more low riders, or more tricks with mirrors. But to street rodders, Oakland is *it*. Thirty years ago it was a hot rod show, and that meant *roadsters*. Today it is a roadster show, and that means *street rods*."

Award, which essentially filled the void left by the Custom d'Elegance Award. Any vehicle in the 1974 show not in the running for the AMBR was considered eligible for the Al Slonaker Award.

Sadly, shortly after the 1975 show, Al Slonaker died of respiratory problems. His death prompted Baggy to change the name of the Al Slonaker Award to the Al Slonaker Memorial Award. To this day it is presented to the car judged to have the most innovative craftsmanship and engineering applied to its design. Next to the AMBR, the Al Slonaker Memorial Award is the oldest presentation that the Grand National Roadster Show hands out.

Another key personality from the show's early years lost his life in 1974. Mel Fernandez, Al Slonaker's right-hand man at Oakland and who, for years, also served as the official starter for various race tracks, was killed while performing his flagman duties during a sprint car race at nearby Calistoga. He was fatally injured when a race car accidentally hit him at the start/finish line.

Despite these setbacks, the Oakland show went on. Practically from the get-go Baggy proved to be the driving force behind the new management team, and he quickly instilled a progressive attitude among the workers and car owners. Baggy's first order of business was to create a more orderly manner in how the show cars were displayed during show hours.

"When I bought Oakland, there were lawn chairs and stuff in the displays," he said in reference to the casual manner in which the car owners lounged around their vehicles during show time. Baggy's new rule stated simply: the only thing in the display would be the cars and a few *acceptable* show props. "Every show is different," observes

America's Most Beautiful Roadster of 1975 went to Lonnie Gilbertson of Portland, Oregon. This is the only double winner in two configurations, 1971 and 1975. He re-did his '23 Ford roadster, with a Gary Crisp yellow pearl mural paint job. The engine was a 327-ci '68 Chevy with a blower, and a custom set of headers that exited just in front of the rear wheels.

Baggy, adding, "People came to see the cars at Oakland." Proclaimed Baggy: the spectators did not come to view car owners sprawled, swigging a beer, in their lawn chairs next to the cars.

Also, the Baggy dictum stated that car displays had to be tasteful and straightforward in their presentation. Again,

From Fremont, California, Howdy Ledbetter came with his '32 Ford Tudor sedan. Its Himsl & Haas paint job was very colorful, including reds, oranges, browns, and white. The complete undercarriage was chromed. Peeking out from the hood is the blown 350-ci Chevy engine. The tranny was a Turbo automatic leading to a Jaguar rear end. Wire wheels were Borranis wrapped with Goodyear rubber.

Bill Roach of Concord, California, came up with a winner with his '27 T roadster body on a frame made of 4130 chromemoly tubing. Pete Odgen fitted the aluminum belly pan, hood, nose, and hand-formed grille. The entire drivetrain was from a Ford Pinto, a popular modification during hot rodding in the '70s. The wire wheels were from a Ford Thunderbird and the red Naugahyde upholstery by Ken Foster.

The 1975 owners of this '40 Mercury convertible four-door sedan were Louie Martin and Dennis Nash. Bertolucci's Body Shop of Sacramento, California, chopped the windshield four inches, and made a removable hardtop in the process. The hood was nosed and extended to meet the '46 Chevy grille, the headlights frenched, and the bumpers pirated from a '42 Chevy. The 276-ci '42 Mercury flathead packed an Iskenderian cam and Edelbrock heads.

From T to 1932, Andy Brizio built another outstanding roadster. This is how it looked at Oakland in 1975. The engine was a Douglas Engineering balanced 350-ci '73 Chevy with an Andy's combination blower and Mallory ignition. The exhaust headers were custom made, and the Turbo 400 spooled itself to a '70 Jaguar rear end. Disc brakes and Zenith chrome wires with Goodyear tires were mounted at all four corners.

this was to better showcase the cars. A simple display, reasoned Baggy, offered few distractions for the people walking the aisles. Recently Baggy told of one incident years ago about a 1938 Chevrolet. According to Baggy the owner had positioned several bright spotlights in the car's interior, in hopes of giving his display more pizzazz. Baggy saw it as creating a distraction for the car and other entries. Said Baggy about the blinding lights, "We yanked them out."

If you get the impression that Baggy was hard-nosed, hear him when he says: "I had no gray zones." In short, there were two options that a car owner could exercise at the "new" Oakland—the Baggy way, or the no way. Like he said, there would be no gray zones.

Baggy also commanded a tight fiscal ship, and almost immediately he began trimming what could be considered excess fat from the show's format. One of the early trimmings was the model car show that was traditionally held in conjunction with the main event. For years this sideshow allowed the entrants to purchase a two-for-one ticket that allowed them to come to the car show (with their model car that would be displayed the duration of the event), then

Dean Jeffries, from Hollywood, California, attended the 1975 show with his *Mantaray*, a hand-built custom that won the Tournament of Fame in 1964. This time it sported a new paint job of pearl yellow and multi-hued reds, limes, and oranges. The engine was a Ford Fairlane 289 with Cobra racing modifications by Carroll Shelby, nestled inside a prewar Grand Prix Maseratti chassis that retained its 15-inch finned drum brakes.

Joe Ross, known as "Joe The Chromer" from Salinas, California, owned this pearl yellow '23 T roadster pickup. The engine was a 427-ci Ford with NASCAR-type intake and a pair of Holley 600-cfm carbs. Outside type headers had built in mufflers. Bill Manger of Castroville, California, did the brown top and Naugahyde upholstery. The wheel/tire combo included Firestone skins on Zenith wires.

The last of my 1975 pictures shows John Buttera's '26 T Ford Tudor sedan. It's stock -looking—sort of—but under the hood is a 289-ci '67 Ford engine. Power goes through a B & M transmission to a modified XKE "John-uar" rear end. The interior was finished in tan and brown by noted upholsterer Tony Nancy. The Chesterfield Brown paint was applied by the late Steve Archer. Goodyear tires were on Boranni wire wheels.

return on Sunday to retrieve their model and award.

Baggy changed that. "It got out of hand," he said years later. "People would bring in a (model) car just to get a comeback ticket for Sunday. We stopped that." Another gray zone was erased from Oakland. There would be more, such as, The Battle of the Bands. This non-automotive sideshow happened to be a survivor of the 1960s, and like the name suggested, it was a contest among rock 'n' roll bands to see who could play the best—or the loudest—at the car shows. To be sure, the Battle of the Bands became a mainstay at car shows across the country, and in some shows, it was considered an institution. That is, until Baggy pulled the plug at Oakland.

"I stopped them," he points out. Reason: As Baggy puts it as only Baggy can, "They played *too* *&(*&^%@#$ loud!" Of course, there was business logic behind his decision to go unplugged. The vendors were beginning to complain that the noise and large crowds standing and watching the battling bands interfered with sales on the floor. Baggy was in tune with the vendors, recognizing that they were more important to the show than the non-automotive-related rock bands, which he deemed expendable.

"When I stopped them (Battle of the Bands), everybody (other promoters) in the United States stopped them," he said. While the sounds of silence became music to Baggy's ears, in truth the tune he played as the show's new producer helped re-establish the true existence of car shows such as Oakland, and that was to display some of the finest hot rods and customs in the world—not to provide an audition session for pop bands.

Here's a pair of typical traditional hot rods that belonged to Darrell Packard and the late Bill Burnham. Packard's was the yellow '29 Ford roadster with a 327-ci Chevy engine under the Hagemann-built three-piece hood. It sports a brown Naugahyde and fabric interior. In traditional fashion, the wishbones were split and chromed, and the roadster rides on big and little tires. Next to it is *Old Blue*, Burnham's famous '29 Ford roadster. And behind *Old Blue* sits another famous roadster, Brian Burnett's AMBR of 1979.

Dick Megugorac—better known as Magoo—is famous for his '29 Ford highboys. Pictured here is his Model A roadster on narrowed '32 rails at the '79 show. The engine was a 327-ci Chevy, linked to a Turbo 350 tranny and a '64 Ford rear end. Magoo's wife, Lois, stitched the red Naugahyde and fabric interior. Lem Tolliver's yellow '29 is to the right.

Don't think that Baggy was simply in it for the car enthusiasts, though. He was a businessman first, foremost and always, so he kept a vigilant eye on the most important part of the show equation, and that was the bottom line. Immediately, he pointed his efforts toward bolstering the number of cars at the Oakland Coliseum, where the show relocated in 1968. "Oakland was a very small show when I took it over," he said.

One way to bolster the number of entries was to expand the floor space, so he convinced the Coliseum's

The 1979 AMBR of Brian Burnett's, affectionately known as *Deucari*, is a unique '32 Ford roadster—it was powered by a 245-ci V-12, twin overhead cam Ferrari engine that was fed by a trio of Weber two-barrel carbs. To accommodate the engine's two distributors, the firewall was recessed and smoothed. The chromed Boranni rims maintain the classy Italian theme. The black roadster to the right is an old Magoo-built '29 Ford on a Deuce frame.

management to allow the cars to be displayed in the sports arena as well as the catacomblike underground Exposition Hall that connected the arena to the outdoor baseball stadium. The benefit was an increase in the number of hot rods and customs displayed during the 1977 show, from 110 vehicles to 170.

The move into the adjoining arena required a change in show dates, too, that took into account the game dates reserved by the arena's primary tenant, the NBA Golden State Warriors basketball team. Years later, 1997 and 1998 to be precise, extenuating circumstances forced the Coliseum management to take away the show's traditional dates, forcing the Grand National Roadster Show to relocate to temporary facilities (two tents, in 1997) outside the Coliseum and—of all places—San Francisco (in 1998; more about that in Chapter 5: 1990–1998).

Today, eight years after selling his interest in the Grand National Roadster Show to the show's current owner, Don Tognotti, Baggy gruffly points out the Coliseum's lack of foresight, "Where are the Warriors now? In last place, that's where."

Baggy has no lost love for the owner of the Oakland Raiders, the NFL football team that leases the stadium, either. About Al Davis, Baggy once said, "He keeps threatening to move," indicating that the Roadster Show has always been a dependable and worthy tenant, while Davis has rarely displayed firm roots or loyalty to the city that, for years, has been known as Raidertown.

Baggy also maintained close affection for celebrities who helped promote his show through the years. Celebrities, Baggy points out, play a key role in helping bolster the show's attendance, so he never backed away from hiring famous personalities to showcase on Oakland's marquee. Baggy's favorite celebrity, the one who displayed the most loyalty to the Grand National Roadster Show, was major league baseball star Reggie Jackson.

Fittingly, Jackson is a car guy who has owned literally hundreds of cars during the past 20 or so years. One year, while Jackson was a member of the Oakland Athletics baseball team, Baggy hired him to help promote the show. The future Hall of Famer was asked to attend the show and sign autographs, which he did for his normal appearance fee. It was a typical business deal, the kind that both Baggy and Jackson were familiar with. It just so happened that the same year Jackson was in the midst of negotiating his contract with the Athletics; neither side could agree on a salary, so talks were at a stalemate. Naturally, the local press treated the situation as a major news story, and they hounded Jackson for a comment while he was working for Baggy at the Oakland show. Jackson, who one day would earn the moniker Mr. October, held firm, refusing to discuss baseball at that time. He cordially told the press, in so many words, "I'm here for Mr. Bagdasarian. He's paying me to be here for his car show, not to discuss my baseball career."

"I knew at that moment," recalls Baggy years later, "that he was an honorable man."

Despite Baggy's iron-fisted rule as a show administrator, he could not dictate the styling trends and fashions that evolved during the remainder of the 1970s. The decade was rife with curious fads, too. It was an unforgettable time, even if you weren't tuned in to the car show scene. Clothing styles centered around unisex fashions such as patchwork vests, flared pants and square-toed platform shoes. Men unabashedly wore polyester leisure suits adorned with white belts and shoes, and women could be found parading the streets in miniskirts and knee-high boots, and flashing false eyelashes. It was as if the entire country had been smitten by the Brady Bunch.

Closer to the car scene, the van movement was in full swing by the middle of that decade and their popularity spread to the Grand National Roadster Show, too. Soon the Oakland Coliseum was awash with vans adorned in colorful murals painted on their slab sides and flat tops.

The van movement prompted others to join in the free-for-all. As the decade progressed, the Coliseum's show floor became cluttered with customized speed boats, minibikes, choppers, and dune buggies sporting colorful paint jobs and gobs of chrome. It looked like someone declared open season on specialized vehicles, and Oakland was ground zero.

The hot rodders responded with their own psychedelic paint jobs that were based on painting techniques originally

From Redding, California, came Jim and Louise Collins with their '32 Ford phaeton. Under the hood sat a 327-ci Chevy with a Gilmer-driven 4-71 supercharger and Holley double-pumper carb. The remainder of the drivetrain included a Turbo 400 transmission and a 'Vette rear end with 3.08 gears. Kustom Kolors in Redding applied the Firemist Cadillac Blue paint. The handsome interior sports blue leather from Scotland. The top's fabric is from Mercedes Benz stock.

pioneered by customizers of the 1950s and 1960s. Among the painters from those early times was Larry Watson, who fostered such avant-garde techniques as glow paints and flip-flop colors, seaweed flames and spider webs. These and other painting tricks eventually were explored in depth by painters of the 1970s, all searching for something wilder, more psychedelic than what others before them had tried.

No doubt, the profile of the custom car world had changed. By the end of the decade lead sleds were a thing of the past, hot rods were no longer considered pieces of affordable transportation that any teenager could build for a few bucks, and chopper motorcycles, vans, and other oddball vehicles constituted the bulk of the Oakland Roadster Show's entry lists. The trickle-down even had a pronounced effect on *Hot Rod* magazine, which began devoting a majority of its editorial space to vans and pick-up trucks, even high-powered speed boats.

Hot rod roadsters? Well, they still could be found on the streets and at the shows, but not in such plentiful numbers as the early days of the first Oakland shows. The show scene in the Bay Area was changing, and by the next decade a new generation of builders would emerge. The new blood would bring with them a new spirit that would blend new ideas with past traditions and styles. The emergence of this new generation would change for-

Gary Arias of Niles, California, showed up at Oakland in 1979 with this neat little '29 Ford roadster. The bright red paint and bodywork were by Joe Contreras, and noted Bay Area upholsterer Howdy's of Fremont stitched the black Naugahyde interior. The hood and side panels boast 45 louvers, and the remainder of the coach work is adorned with gold pinstriping.

ever the way the world viewed hot rodding. Indeed, the metamorphosis would prove so profound that, today, it appears as though the new trends and styles will last into the next millennium when the Grand National Roadster Show begins its second 50 years as America's oldest hot rod car show.

From nearby Concord, California, came this sweet chopped '32 Ford five-windowed coupe, belonging to Dan Pimentel. Other bodywork features a filled grille shell, and molded cowl air vent. Gold pinstriping adorns both the body and steel wheels. The interior was finished with custom bucket style seats trimmed in cloth fabric.

1980–1989
The Renaissance Years

Between 1967 and 1987, famed custom-car builder Joe Bailon had been to the Grand National Roadster Show exactly one time. That was in 1972 when he made a brief appearance, in the process collecting one of his nine Custom d'Elegance awards, this one based on a 1965 Chevrolet that he smoothed and formed into a thing of beauty.

It wasn't until 1987, when Bailon was honored as the grand show's Builder of the Year that he came back in full force. As recipient of the newly instituted award, Bailon brought with him a small squadron of show cars. He stated years later, "I returned to Oakland with five really bitchin' customs."

Having received the inaugural Builder of the Year award in 1987, Bailon left Oakland that year a reborn man, one with a new purpose in his role as the custom car world's elder statesman. Bailon had decided that *he* would be the one to rekindle America's love for his first love, and that was low-riding custom cars. Actually, Bailon's campaign to revive the customs began the moment he arrived at the 1987 Grand National Roadster Show. As he strolled through the Oakland Coliseum that year he was shocked at what he saw. Spread before him on the arena floor were vehicles he wasn't used to seeing at shows such as Oakland. "It was full of pickups that you could walk under," he says

The 1989 AMBR winner, Ermie Immerso of Rancho Dominguez, California. His 1925 T *Golden Star* wowed everybody again in 1991. Immerso won his first AMBR the previous year with his '32 Ford roadster. *Golden Star's* engine was based on a 255-ci aluminum 1965 dry sump Ford DOHC Indy motor. It was dressed for show with a hand-built manifold to hold four Weber 48 IDA carbs. The striking orange pearl paint was by Don Thelan, and the candy flames and striping were by Dennis Ricklefs. Vic Kitchens did the Naugahyde upholstery. I took this picture in 1991.

The 1981 AMBR winner was John Siroonian of Fresno, California. Built by the late Don Thelan of Buffalo Motor Cars, Siroonian's Deuce was painted a dynamic Candy Red lacquer. The luxurious sculpted seats were upholstered with tan Naugahyde, and the supercharged Gurney-Weslake Ford engine was polished throughout. The entire undercarriage is chromed, and the Halibrand wheels and Championship rear end were polished. A full mirror display shows off the chromed-and-polished underpinnings. Street Rodder *magazine*

with disgust in reference to the assembled mass of four-wheel-drive vehicles on display. "Boats and motorcycles, too. Few customs." The old soldier of the lead-slinging days was aghast. "I couldn't believe it."

Though disappointed, Bailon wasn't discouraged, and he put forth a determined effort to lead a revival of a style of car that helped make Oakland the grandest show of them all back in the 1950s. Almost immediately after

Don Varner's *California Star* was crafted from 4130 chromemoly tubing for its space frame. The chassis has a Lotus-type race suspension featuring independent front and rear units. Cantilevered A-arms and Spax coil over shocks comprise the front suspension. Steering is a narrowed Porsche 911 rack-and-pinion assembly, and the turbocharged 60-degree Chevy V-6 was built by Cub Barnett. *Don Varner*

Bailon returned home, he picked up the telephone and called his friends, the custom car owners. He told them that their hibernation was over, and that they should make plans for an appearance with their cars at the 1988 show.

"So I got some of the West Coast Kustoms to bring some of their cars," he said. "That started the customs again." Today he proudly boasts, "Now you don't see a whole bunch of tall pickups (at Oakland) anymore. So I feel I had a little to do with it (reviving Oakland to its former status and glory)."

Clearly, the return of the customs capped a period in which the Oakland show underwent a renaissance like it had never experienced before. As Oakland's old guard began its phase-out during the 1970s, the show headed into strange waters, and for a brief period the journey seemed to be leading nowhere. Then, as if to celebrate the new decade, Oakland charted a new course in the 1980s. The journey once again had purpose.

Several factors played a leading role in this renaissance. Foremost was the blending of old and new blood with the people who created the cars for the show. Fittingly, this blending of ages showed up at the 1980 Grand National Roadster Show when a former AMBR winner, John Corno (whose rear-engine Model A won in 1972), delivered another winning candidate for the nine-foot trophy. Corno won his second AMBR with another Model A, this time a 1928 highboy that was the product of some of the craftiest designers and fabricators in the industry who, it turned out, were beginning to establish their own reputations in the hot rod world. Corno's crew included Harry Bradley, Steve Davis, Mike McKennett, and John Buttera.

Actually, Corno's 1928 highboy roadster utilized a styling technique that Lil' John Buttera had developed several years earlier. Using bits and pieces of scrap aluminum billet, Lil' John had machined and filed and whittled parts that, when they left his machine shop, looked especially unique and different than anything anybody else had on their hot rods. Buttera's style came to be known as the "high tech" look, but in reality Lil' John says that he built his own parts because it was cheaper for him to do so, and after all, reasons the veteran machinist, building precision parts is what he was trained to do in the first place. As he once stated so simply and matter-of-factly about his skills as a machinist, "That's what I do."

In truth, Lil' John did more than simply machine chunks of aluminum into high-tech hot rod parts. By putting his talents to work he started a new trend in hot rod building, one that opened the door for a new generation of builders. The new-wave designers, builders, and fabricators include some of today's hot rod greats. Thom Taylor, Chip Foose, Don Thelan, Roy Brizio, Chuck Lombardo, Ron Covell, and Boyd Coddington, to name a few, owe, in part, some of their success to Buttera's pioneering work with the lathe and mill.

The *California Star* was Oakland's AMBR for 1984. Sitting behind the wheel is owner Don Varner; sitting shotgun is master metalworker Ron Covell, who built the aluminum body and components. Before Covell began fabricating the body, a full-scale mock-up was made from meticulous drawings, then glued to the outside of a '27 T roadster to get the desired shape. Finally, Bob Acosta applied the rich-looking Ferrari red lacquer paint. *Don Varner*

Thelan and his Buffalo Motor Cars shop was the first to capitalize on those talents, building the 1981 AMBR winner for John Siroonian (yet *another* AMBR recipient from Fresno, California). Siroonian's entry was a '32 Ford highboy that had a supercharged Gurney-Weslake Ford engine. The highboy's candy red paint job waxed eloquent for the high-tech look, giving builders something to aim for in 1982.

Coddington scored the bull's-eye the next year, building a winner for Jamie Musselman. Musselman's entry was especially unique among AMBR winners because it was the first post-1932 year car to win the award. Until then only

Next Page
Viewed from the rear, notice the *California Star*'s engine compartment ventilation that utilizes a grille on top of the rear deck. Exhausts are ducted through a lower louvered panel to the vents. A Lexan windshield shrouds the interior that was upholstered in natural tan Connolly leather by Putman's Interiors of Sacramento. Two quarter-doors open for the passenger and driver to easily get in and out. Radial tires mount on Centerline wheels with knock-off hubs. *Don Varner*

Cloning Around
They Had So Much Fun at the
39th Annual Grand National Roadster Show That
They Held it Twice

There's an old saying that goes something like, "if they liked it once, they'll love it again." And if there's credence to that epigram, then the 39th Annual Grand National Roadster Show is the Oakland that will go down in history as the most loved of all the roadster shows, because there were actually *two* 39th Annual shows—1987 and 1988.

The cloning of No. 39 actually dates back to 1959 when, based on the 1950 show being the inaugural National Roadster Show, Oakland celebrated its 10th anniversary. By all rights, the 1960 show should have been the 11th annual, but the promoters, for some unexplained reason, proclaimed it to be the 12th annual. Thus began the misconception that the show was originally formed in 1949 as a roadster show.

Based on the revised numerical order, the 1961 show should have marked the *13th* annual Roadster Show. Knowing how superstitious car people can be (remember when green race cars were taboo and women in the pits at Indianapolis were considered bad luck?), Al Slonaker elected not to proclaim the anniversary date for the 1961 show. Instead, Slonaker proved just how shrewd a promoter and businessman he could be when he wrote in the souvenir program's welcome page, "Every year since 1949—the same time, the same place—the big show, 'granddaddy' of all auto shows, the National Roadster Show!" Not a word anywhere in the program about the 1961 show being the 13th annual (even though, in reality, it was only the 12th annual that shared the title National Roadster Show). As a result, the show's anniversary date remained one year out of kilter.

In any case, the omission in 1961 opened the door for Slonaker to make another change, this time to the name of the show. And so, for 1962, he added a single word to the show's title; as of 1962 the National Roadster Show became known as the Grand National Roadster Show (in truth *that* year was the 13th annual National Roadster Show!).

The issue of sidestepping the 13th annual celebration eventually melded into obscurity. Not until the 25th anniversary year—1973—did anybody realize the mistake. But by then it was too late, and people, including the show's new promoter Harold "Baggy" Bagdasarian, lived with the misalignment.

That is, until George Martin of the *San Francisco Chronicle* hounded Baggy to correct it. Initially, Baggy said that the error was no big deal. After all, he surmised, every year without fail the show went on, and being the Granddaddy of all shows, Oakland remained the most prestigious on the circuit. Who cared if the annual anniversary date was a year out of synch?

Finally, the persistent Martin dangled a tantalizingly tasty carrot that Baggy couldn't refuse to snap up. As Baggy explained years later, "He said, 'Correct that, and I'll give you half a page in the Green Section free,' so I did." Anybody who knows Baggy also knows that he's a crafty businessman, one who never lets a good deal slip through his hot little hands. So Baggy made the correction—which cost him nothing—and he got his half-page ad—which also cost him nothing—in the daily newspaper's special classified section.

Baggy made his one-for-the-money/two-for-the-show switch in 1987 and 1988 when both shows were given the esteemed honor as the 39th Annual Grand National Roadster Show. Nobody seemed to mind the redundancy in '88 because nobody seemed to notice the duplicity in the first place. It was, as the great baseball legend Yogi Berra once said, "*dé jà vu* all over again." In fact, not even the enthusiast publications made note of the cloning during their 1988 show reports.

None of that really mattered, though, because people at the '88 show had just as much fun at the second 39th annual Oakland as they did at the first 39th. Which just goes to show, you can never have *two* much fun at the Grand National Roadster Show!

1932, Model A, and Model T Fords had scooped the honor. Designer Thom Taylor based Musselman's winner on a 1933 Ford fenderless roadster. It was a typical early-Coddington exercise, too, emphasizing a smooth, seamless look, what he termed "hiccupless."

Lombardo's crew at California Street Rods was the next new-age builder to win, snapping up the 1983 trophy with a simple, yet well-executed Deuce highboy design. The following year, 1984, the AMBR winner was a rather radical roadster, designed by Don Varner, and hammered into shape from sheet aluminum by master metalsmith Ron Covell. The basis of the project was a Ford Model T, but you'd never know it by looking at the sleek roadster. Varner called his entry the *California Star*, and it shone brightly until the next year when another Thom Taylor-designed/Boyd Coddington-built car won. This car, crafted for Larry and Judie Murray, was another 1933 Ford, what many termed a "phantom phaeton," because it was actually a four-seater open-top that originally started life at the Ford factory as a sedan.

Thelan's shop returned to the top in 1986 with a '33 Ford roadster built for Jim McNamara. The following year it was Roy Brizio's turn as master builder, when he shoehorned a Ferrari V-12 engine into a Deuce chassis for James Ells. In the process Brizio joined his father, Andy Brizio, as the only father/son combo on Oakland's elite AMBR honor roll of builders.

As the decade neared an end, the 1980s AMBR top 10 was topped by a single man, Ermie Immerso, with back-to-back winners in 1988 and 1989. Immerso became the third man to achieve this feat (Richard Peters won two in a row with *Ala Kart* in 1958 and 1959, and Bob Reisen's twin-engine *Invader* duplicated that honor in 1967 and 1968), but he was the first double-winner using two different roadsters. Immerso's first AMBR car was an immaculate full-fendered Deuce that sported an Ardun V-8 and traditional Ford running gear. As happened exactly 10 years before with Phil Cool's Deuce highboy, the hot rod community proclaimed Immerso's Thelan-built traditional-style roadster a return to normalcy.

Immerso discredited those soothsayers in 1989 when he rolled a tricked-out track-T roadster into the Oakland arena. The flamed roadster was powered by a Ford-Cosworth V-8 motor that Immerso snatched from an aging Indianapolis race car. The exotic double-overhead camshaft race car engine was dressed with chrome- and gold-plated parts, and the entire car was finished with the same methodical detail that helped Andy Brizio win the big trophy in 1970 with his *Instant T* kit car.

The shift in roadster design was only part of the change that Oakland experienced during the 1980s. As the "Me Decade" unfolded, many baby boomers were approaching middle age, which also meant they were hir-

Oakland in 1986, from the scrapbook of Tom Cutino: Here is a montage of some of Cutino's snapshots. The top picture shows Cutino on the freeway coming from the town of Rio Vista, California, going to the show. The bottom left picture shows his location on the arena floor of the Coliseum. The lower picture to the right shows Cutino after his chopped '50 Ford was cleaned up. *Tom Cutino*

ting full stride in their professional careers. Bolstered by more income than ever, and relieved of many financial obligations now that they were also becoming empty nesters, the gearhead baby boomers found themselves in a unique situation. They now had plenty of disposable income. It was money that they could funnel—in large portions—into hobbies and other distractions such as hot rods and custom cars. Across the country car collections grew. It was at that time, too, that many middle-aged hot rodders realized that their hobby had roots. Often those roots led to old hot rods that had been neglected over time. Armed with more money than ever, the baby boomers marched forth, buying and restoring many of those old hot rods. By decade's end nostalgia became the buzz-word used by baby boomers all across the nation.

Among the first of the oldies cars to re-emerge onto the show scene was a 1957 Chrysler custom that was originally hammered into shape by expert bodyman Joe Wilhelm two decades before. Famed painter and flame-artist Rod Powell was responsible for the reincarnation of this jewel, unveiling it at the 1982 Grand National Roadster Show.

Within a few years, old hot rods and customs were being recycled at a rapid rate. Many of the restored hot rods weren't necessarily landmark cars, either. For example, Greg Borrelli showed up at Oakland '87 with a revived '32 Ford roadster once owned by Tex Smith. The car, called *Old Marvin* by Tex during the car's heyday, was restored and readied for Oakland. Borrelli beamed with joy when he rolled the full fendered Deuce onto the show floor that year.

James Ells of South San Francisco wanted the '32 Ford roadster of his dreams. Roy Brizio Street Rods made that dream come true. In six months' time Brizio and Ells turned out what you see here. Its eye-catching Ferrari Red paint job is complemented by an equally noticeable V-12 engine that was snatched from a 1971 Ferrari. Naturally, the Ferrari's five-speed transmission was included in the deal, and to maintain the performance theme Brizio slipped in a Halibrand Champ quick change rear end. Even though this car was the AMBR in 1987, I took this picture at Oakland in 1990 when the car was on display.

Accompanying him on the oldies chart in 1987 was John Slaughter, who had acquired and refurbished John Corno's 1972 AMBR winner, the fabled rear-engine Model A.

Nostalgia reigned supreme the next year at Oakland as the show headed back to the future when Dream Cars showed off a 1932 Ford three-window coupe that looked as if it drove right out of 1955. The black beauty had a traditionally built flathead V-8 engine, and wide whitewall bias-ply tires. The seed for building traditional-style hot rods had been planted, and boomers no longer had to only dream about days gone past. Now they could build hot rods that resembled the rides that they enjoyed as kids so many years ago.

In 1989 Mickey Himsl led the nostalgia parade when he displayed a beautiful Model T roadster that was powered by a flathead V-8. Himsl's roadster had an interesting, even somber, past; originally it began life as a hot rod in 1948, shortly before the outbreak of the Korean War. Unfortunately, Hal Zieska, the young man who undertook the project, was drafted into the army before he could finish the car. Worse yet, he was killed in combat, and for many years after his death the half-finished car sat in the family's garage, as if enshrined in the son's memory. Finally, in 1985, Himsl acquired the incomplete roadster. As if a tribute to the young man who started the project so many years ago, Himsl completed the roadster as it would have been built in 1950. It was truly a fitting eulogy to Hal Zieska and his love for hot rodding.

The "Me Decade" signed off with several other cars from the past that were put under the Oakland Coliseum's nostalgia spotlight. Among the oldies at the 1989 show was a 1941 Ford pickup rebuilt by Cal Carnahan that boasted bodywork from Valley Customs, a shop that was short-lived but noted for its many customs in the 1950s. Also on display was the 1960 AMBR, *Emperor*, and Darryl Starbird's sleek *Manta Ray*, first shown in 1964.

And if those cars didn't push your old-time nostalgia button, Bruce Glascock showed a Model A roadster at the 1989 Oakland show that he had located on Catalina Island, a resort island located about 26 miles from Los Angeles. The old 1950s-vintage highboy hot rod sported the same faded yellow paint, '40 Ford steering wheel, bobbed rear fenders, even the rust and dust, as when Glascock first spotted it shortly before the show that year.

The show management was swept by the nostalgia wave during the 1980s, too. Recognizing that the show had roots that reached to a glorious past, the promoters capitalized on Oakland's history by reinstituting the Hall of Fame, which was originally formed in 1960, only to wither on the vine by 1967.

A driving force behind the Hall of Fame's return in 1988 was former AMBR winner Don Tognotti (1964; *King T*). Tognotti joined the show in 1987 when he bought out Darryl Starbird's share. Buoyed by Harold Bagdasarian's seniority and experience, and invigorated by Tognotti's eagerness, the Grand National Roadster Show enjoyed a vitality and enthusiasm reminiscent of the early days when Oakland was still a novelty among the automotive crowd.

"We just tried to kick back more of the traditional thing (of the show)," Tognotti said about bringing back the Hall of Fame, and in recognizing the Builder of the Year, a special presentation that was established in 1987. Adds Tognotti, "It's a big thing to be in the Hall of Fame."

Perhaps Tognotti could have expanded that statement to include the entire show, because as the 1990s approached, the Grand National Roadster Show grew in quality and popularity. Oakland's fifth decade, people would learn, was to be a period in which the show grew in size, stature, and significance to the automotive world in general, and to the custom car world in particular.

Perhaps Bagdasarian puts it best, "Life changes every six hours. You better know how to change with it." Time had proven once again that the Grand National Roadster Show knows how to change with time. And, as everyone was to find out, the 1990s would be a time of dynamic change.

GRAND NATIONAL ROADSTER SHOW

HALL of FAME

First 100 Members

1960 *Charter Members*
Al Slonaker (President), Oakland
Joe Bailon, Auburn
George Barris, N. Hollywood
Mrs. Harold Casaurang, Concord
Ezra Ehrhardt
Romeo Palamides, Oakland
Wally Parks, Glendale
Robert E. Petersen
Eric Rickman, Hacienda Heights
Gordon Vann, Berkeley
Walt Woron

1961
Chic Cannon, Templeton
Dick Day
Fred Esser, Cottonwood
Blackie Gejeian, Fresno
Howard Leever, San Diego
Richard Peters, Fresno
Guy Root
Gene Winfield, Canoga Park

1962
Bob Accosta, Fremont
Harold Bagdasarian, Sacramento
Jack Hagemann Sr., Alamo
Dean Moon, Los Angeles
Jerry Sahagon, Concord
Mary Slonaker, Scottsdale, AZ
Joe Wilhelm, San Jose
Lee Wood, San Leandro
Jerry Woodward, Provo, UT

1963
Donald Bell, Hayward
Bill Cushenbery, Bakersfield
Ted Frye, Los Angeles
Frank Livingston, San Leandro
Bob McNulty
A.K. Miller, Whittier
Barbara Parks, Glendale
Leroi "Tex" Smith, Driggs, ID
Darryl Starbird, Afton, OK

1964
Paul Bender, Modesto
E. J. "Bud" Coons, Groove, OK
Mel Fernandes, Castro Valley
Richard Guasco, Pleasanton
Tommy "The Greek" Hrones, Oakland
Dean Jeffries, W. Hollywood
Spencer Murray, La Canada
Joe Ortiz, Groveland
Bob Tindle, Portland

1965
Fred Agabashian, Sacramento
Tony Del Rio, Hayward
Mike Homen, Seaside
Beverly Johnson
Kenny Levenberg
Wilbert "Sonny" Morris, Fremont
William Penland, Alamo
Don Tognotti, Sacramento
Harry Costa, Burlingame

1966
Andy Brizio, Concord
Ray Brock, El Segundo
Carl Casper, Louisville, KY
Joe Cruces, Chico
Jim Giminez, Hayward
Don Lokey, Fresno
Chuck Trantham, Oregon House
Bob Larivee, Pontiac, MI
Dave Puhl

1988
Roy Brizio, S. San Francisco
Boyd Coddington, Anaheim
Dick Dean, Riverside
Frank DeRosa, Pittsburg
Rod Powell, Salinas

1989
Tom Medley, Burbank
Bud Millard, Millbrae
Arlen Ness, Castro Valley

1990
Ken Foster, Sacramento
Norm Grabowski, Lead Hill
Tom Prufer, Lakewood

1991
Jack Hagemann Jr., Morgan Hill
Andy Southard Jr., Salinas
Richard Zocchi, Walnut Creek

1992
Kent Fuller, Canoga Park
Art Himsl, Concord
Hank Medeiros, Hayward
Bill Reasoner, Walnut Creek
Ray Smith, Walnut Creek

1993
Mike Alexander, Detroit, MI
Larry Alexander, Detroit, MI
Gray Baskerville, Los Angeles
Von Dutch, Los Angeles
Bill Hines, Garden Grove
Rick Perry, Galt
Greg Sharp, La Mirada

1994
Gil Ayala, Paramont
Bill Burnham, Alamo
Hershel Conway, Bell Gardens
Howdy Ledbetter, Fremont

1995
Sam Barris, Roseville
John D'Agostino, Antioch
Sam Foose, Solvang
Rich Pichette, Moreno Valley

1996
Bob Cecchini, San Leandro
Steve Moal, Oakland

** *First year*
* *No Hall of Fame 1967 thru 1987*

If you ever want to know who the first 100 inductees were to the Grand National Roadster Show's Hall Of Fame, look here. This plaque commemorates the first 100 members. It was given to each member as a memento of their induction date. Charter membership started in 1960, and the Hall of Fame lasted through 1966 and was suspended the following year. It resumed again in 1988 and continues through today, becoming an integral part of the greatest custom car show on earth. I'm proud to say that I was inducted in 1991 with Jack Hagemann Jr. and Richard Zocchi. It is indeed an honor to be a member. I received this plaque in 1996.

5

1990–1998
The High-Dollar Years

The prosperity enjoyed in the 1980s spilled right into the 1990s, as the Grand National Roadster Show continued to grow in size and stature. The glory days of Oakland had certainly returned, but a basic fact remained: fewer and fewer hot rod *roadsters* were actually entered or displayed in the very show that derived its name—indeed, its very existence—from these cars.

By 1994 the situation was clear, and desperate. The Grand National Roadster Show had become, in truth, a Grand National *Custom Car* Show. Wrote Mike Bishop for *American Rodder* magazine in his 1994 show report:

"Once again, Oakland both delights and disappoints. The delight is in the high quality of entries accepted for this prestigious old-timer of hot rod showcasing. But the Grand National Roadster Show disappoints in the paucity of roadsters. With only nine roadsters in the main arena, there may be a legitimate argument here about truth in ballyhoo."

The ballyhoo was shared by the promoters and the automotive press alike. Certainly the show promoters were excited about the number of entries. At 300—and rising every year—the Grand National Roadster Show had emerged from the 1980s as one of the largest indoor custom car shows in the country. Due to its size, and the quality of cars vying for awards, the automotive press couldn't ignore Oakland, either, making it mandatory on the hot rod magazines' annual whistle-stop tour of event

Moonfire is the name of Frank and Kathy Livingston's custom '49 Mercury. Paul Bragg of Paso Robles, California, did the metalwork, chopping the top, forming the grille opening and grille, setting the custom taillights, etc. He also installed the Buick Apollo sub-frame, Olds 350 engine, and '69 Trans Am rear end. Jerry Sahagon did the interior in Naugahyde and cloth, selecting cool-looking ice-white and aqua colors. When it came to the paint, the Livingstons had Bill Reasoner do the light pearl aqua blue color.

Butch Martino of White Plains, New York, was the 1990 AMBR winner. Other awards at Oakland include Best Rod, Best in Class (radical altered roadster), Best in Show, and, of course, the prestigious AMBR title. Inspired by a design penned by Thom Taylor, Hot Rods by Boyd performed all the meticulous work. The body was formed from aluminum, then covered with plum-colored lacquer. The sanitary interior was trimmed with gray Naugahyde and fabric, and a 1989 Corvette V-8 was wedged beneath the smooth hood.

One of the cars in the upstairs rotunda during the 1990 Oakland show was William C. Turner's 1947 Ford coupe. The top was mildly chopped, the headlights frenched, and the hood nosed and louvered. In addition, the taillights were frenched, and the trunk smoothed. For power, Turner elected to use a late-model 302-ci Ford V-8. Who can argue with the rich-looking Champagne lacquer paint?

Tom and Janice Otis, originally from New York, have been "California-ized," if you judge by their hot rods. Just check out their bright red '23 Ford Model T speedster. The engine is a 350/350 drivetrain linked to a sassy Jaguar rear end. There's lots of chrome, too, and a nice gray Naugahyde interior to match. Tom is a member of the L.A. Roadsters and an outstanding flame painter and pinstriper.

At the 1990 show sat *Goldie*, a highly customized '48 Ford replica coupe (made of fiberglass) customized by Gene Winfield for Don Siglar of Pasadena, California. The roof was chopped and a two-inch section came out of the body. Under the hood sat a 350-ci Chevy packing a B & M supercharger. Dan Miller did the honey-colored Naugahyde interior, while Winfield himself applied the striking 14-karat gold color lacquer.

coverages. Truly, as the 1990s unfolded, the enthusiast magazines paid more and more attention to the annual Oakland show.

Underscoring how critical the thinning roadster ranks had become, the 1991 AMBR recipient was a repeat winner, when Ermie Immerso returned with *Golden Star*, the same 1925 Model T that copped the honor in 1989. Sandwiched in between *Golden Star*'s two AMBR years was the Deuce roadster *Passion*, built by Boyd Coddington for Butch Martino of White Plains, New York. It marked only the eighth time the winner was from out of state (even though the car was built in Coddington's former elaborate facility in Stanton, California).

Moreover, Martino's smoothed Deuce highboy roadster spearheaded a movement by the car builders that took advantage of the new, higher quality paints available to them. The abundance of improved paint toners offered by the leading paint suppliers had sparked a crusade among the custom painters to experiment not only with painting

More than once at Oakland a roadster has been built on a stage for all the world to see, giving spectators an idea about how a typical hot rod is built. In 1990 Roy Brizio (left) of Roy Brizio Street Rods and his crew put together a '32 Ford highboy roadster. By the time the five-day show concluded, the roadster was ready to roll. The fellow with the big smile, ready to take a picture, is Pat Ganahl, at the time editor of *Rod & Custom* magazine. Hmm, wonder if I got in his picture?

For the 1991 show Bob Paige entered his old-style custom '40 Ford coupe. The top had been chopped, the door handles taken off, side trim removed, and headlights frenched to follow the contour of the original chromed rims. Notice the old-style flavor served up by the ripple bumpers and the teardrop fender skirts. Dig the maroon paint job, wide whitewall tires, and Cadillac hubcaps.

techniques, but with color selections. Pat Ganahl, then editor for *Rod & Custom*, was first to make note of this when, in his 1990 Oakland show report, he wrote: "Trends? The color purple. As an apparent surprise to everyone, no less than 13 cars on the main arena floor—including most of the AMBR contenders—came in rich shades of purple paint. Nearly all of them had no other graphics besides the bright color."

By the middle of the new decade the painters were experimenting with all sorts of toners, shades, and pig-

Traditionally, the Hall Of Fame programs have been smaller than the regular show programs. They are given to members and their guests at the Hall Of Fame luncheon on Saturday during the final weekend of the show. Shown here is the 1991 program, when I was inducted. My Hall Of Fame pin sits between the two lower pictures. All inductees also receive a nice parchment certificate stating the date they are inducted. In this photo an additional program cover overlaps from the 1989 show.

An envy of every Mercury-lover is the customized '40 that John D'Agostino built! The fabulous Merc has a chopped top, it's been lowered, the fenders are molded, and it was nosed and decked. All the work was done by Bill Reasoner's Custom Shop in Walnut Creek, California. Old-time goodness is retained under the hood with a 255-ci '48 Ford flathead motor, boasting Offenhauser heads and three carbs. The upholstery is maroon mohair and pearl white Naugahyde; the paint is Black Cherry Pearl by Reasoner.

ments. Cited Bishop in his 1996 report for *America Rodder*: "And everywhere there was lots of talk—and excitement—about color this year. As one wag remarked, 'It looks like they lost the red recipe. Thank God!' Mixed in with some wonderful '50s pastels were vibrant, hue-changing pearls, and brilliant candies as expertly laid down as they've ever been. Like proven styling themes, classic paint techniques and colors are always in vogue."

Also coming in vogue—or actually, returning to the forefront of hot rod fashion—were door-slammer customs, in particular those based on 1950s cars. Some of the new-generation customs were built by familiar faces to Oakland. Old-timers such as Joe Bailon, Gene Winfield, and Bill Hines continued to display their handicraft with lay-down customs at the Roadster Show, but the 1990s marked the high point of the next generation of builders and owners, too. As the 1990s rolled on, customizers such as Richard Zocchi, John D'Agostino, Rick Dore, Jimmy Vaughn (the noted blues guitarist), Rich Pichette, and Jimmie Farcello were making names for themselves within the custom car world. In particular, Zocchi and D'Agostino had been a part of the Oakland scene for many years, and like vintage wine their custom cars continued to improve every year. By the 1990s these two men had become the patriarchs of the custom car clan on the West Coast. Oftentimes, these two customizers from the Bay Area showed up with multiple entries at Oakland.

The custom car crowd brought with them more than just a fleet of eye-catching customs to Oakland. Along with their finely sculpted cars came a welcome and refreshing vitality to the show. As Eric Geisert—himself a young aspiring writer making a name for himself in the magazine business—wrote for *Street Rodder* in his 1995 Oakland show report:

Blues guitarist Jimmie Vaughan struck the right chords when he had Gary Howard's shop in Georgetown, Texas, played a tune with this '51 Chevy fastback sedan's sheet metal. Some of the high notes include a 31-tooth Corvette grille, rounded corners on the smoothed hood, frenched headlights, and a sweet-sounding Chevy 350 V-8 playing under the hood. Vaughan calls the car's pearl paint Sweet Baby Lavender. Yeah, sing dem blues!

In 1991, John D'Agostino's *Royal Empress*, a '56 Lincoln hardtop, practically stole the show. The car was chopped four inches by Gene Winfield and featured unusual lowering effects to emphasize the car's long body lines. Additional custom work included shaving the hood, mounting 268 chromed bullets in the custom grille, and dousing the beautiful body with an equally beautiful paint job by custom master Gene Winfield. Sid Chavers stitched in the mohair upholstery, selecting four colors—lavender, platinum, silver, and violet—to accent the car's paint. Awards received were Most Outstanding Custom, Best Paint, and the coveted Al Slonaker Memorial Award for innovation and craftsmanship.

This traditional '32 Ford roadster once belonged to Ed "Axle" Stewart, maker of the Dago Axle. Today it remains in the family, and is owned by son Bob of Pinecove, California. The engine is a 296-ci Mercury flathead with Evans heads and manifold with three Stromberg 48 carburetors. The front axle is an original Dago Axle that was dropped 3 1/2 inches before it was chrome plated. The Cal-Custom hood side panels have 29 louvers. The interior and trunk were trimmed in Oxblood Naugahyde according to Bob's design. The dash holds what Bob describes as five Stewart Warner "Old-Man" gauges, so named because their size makes them easier to read by older men.

Oakland Show 1991. This beautiful Toyota Red '32 Ford roadster belonged to Bob Lockwood of Daly City, California. The roadster originated at Roy Brizio Street Rods, but Lockwood basically built the roadster over a two-year period. Under the hood is a 468-ci Chevy, with a Weiand manifold and four-barrel Holley carb. The louvered hood and side panels are a product of Rootlieb, and the black Naugahyde upholstery was by Sid Chavers.

Jim Davis of Chatsworth, California, and former president of B & M, built a project street rod with this bright red '32 Ford roadster. He finished the car back in 1985. It still exists as seen here in the '91 Oakland Show. Under the hood sat a Chevy with a B & M 250 power charger blower that helped the Bow-Tie motor crank out 540 horsepower at 5,000 rpm!

Always a show that sets the trends instead of following them, it's interesting to watch the resurgence of customs in the rod building world over the past couple of years. John D'Agostino, a perennial show favorite who has shown 18 different cars in the past 25 years at Oakland, had two customs on the arena floor this year. One, named *Golden Starfire*, is a '61 Olds painted a custom gold, and the second was a radical '57 Lincoln, painted in fading greens by Gene Winfield. In addition, John was honored by being inducted into the Oakland Hall of Fame—a select group of individuals who have furthered the rod building cause.

To be sure, the reincarnated Oakland Hall of Fame was gaining a strong foothold within the custom car community, too. When the promoters resurrected the Hall of Fame in 1988, it was as much for a sense of nostalgia for the show as to display their gratitude for the people who helped make Oakland happen in the first place. The Roadster Show's deep-rooted tradition had finally gained the recognition it deserved and earned, and the Hall of Fame transformed into an institution revered by people familiar with the oldest hot rod and custom car show in existence.

Originally, there were 10 charter members to the Hall of Fame, and by 1966 that august body had grown to 64 before the concept was abruptly abandoned in 1967.

Continued on page 103

Another outstanding roadster for 1991 was Gary Matranga's turquoise all-steel-body '32 Ford. This masterpiece was unusual because it had reversed suicide-type doors, hidden hinges, and a built-in windshield with side mirrors. Dennis King of Turlock, California, did the body and paint. The engine is a 410-ci '57 Chrysler with a Bowers blower and Hilborn injector. The hood side panels have hidden tilt-out headlights. The equally stylish black Naugahyde upholstery was by Dave Putman of Sacramento.

Here's an overall view of the Oakland Coliseum during the 1991 show. Looking down onto the arena you'll see the following: Gary Matranga's turquoise-colored '32 Ford roadster; Frank DeRosa's Candy Red customized '40 Mercury coupe to the rear; and DeRosa's purple chopped, channeled, and sectioned '51 Mercury. On the other side of the arena you can see the vendors, such as Roy Brizio Street Rods, who had a roadster and a coupe on display.

Bud Millard of Milbrae, California, owns a Bailon-built chopped '50 Mercury, known as *The Mirage*. The car was chopped 3 1/2 inches in the front and 6 inches in the rear, the hood was nosed and the corners rounded, and Bailon added scoops to the hood sides. The grille opening was modified with a '57 Chevy truck grille, and the front fenders extended 5 inches into frenched headlights and chrome headlight rings. The custom skirts were made from '53 Mercury quarter panels using two Merc spears. The paint is pearl apricot.

Greg Hahn of San Leandro, California, owned this '39 Ford Convertible that started life as a chopped and channeled custom in Pennsylvania back in 1951. Through the years the Ford has changed hands until Hahn obtained it. Surprisingly, the Ford has retained the same '53 Cadillac engine through the years. The chassis was modernized with a Mustang II suspension, and was recently updated with a Packard grille, Candy red paint, and frenched '40s-type headlights.

John Riocabona Jr. of Antioch, California, owned this 1954 Ford Victoria shown here in 1991. Butch Hurlhey of Salinas, California, made a removable chopped top, frenched the headlights, and filled the grille cavity with 20 '54 Chevy grille bars. Maroon front scallops were dressed with red striping around the edges. The white Naugahyde truly reflects the good old days of customizing.

Jim Glymph of Myrtle Beach, South Carolina, drove all the way to Oakland for the 1991 show. He did most of the customizing work on his '56 Chevy hardtop, making it look like it rolled right out of the 1950s. To do that he installed a tube-type grille, nosed the hood, decked the lid, and installed one-piece taillights. Additional oldies add-ons include chrome wheels and lakes pipes down the side. Brother Richard painted the flames, and M. K. John striped the edges.

The last picture from the 1991 Oakland Roadster Show is of this clean '34 Ford three-window coupe owned by B. Gomes. The top has been chopped three inches, and six rows of louvers adorn the hood. I couldn't find much information on this coupe, but it looks as if it has a dropped front axle with aluminum wheels and knock-off caps.

Blue Steel was the name given to Don Raible's 1993 AMBR. As you might guess, the body is steel, originating in Australia, of all places! Terry Hegman worked the body back into shape, and applied the blue/purple urethane paint. Dan Miller finished the interior, using light violet leather with navy blue carpets. Keith Pickrell supplied the all-aluminum 420-ci Donovan big-block motor that was given a show car treatment thanks to gold-plated Weber carbs and magenta valve covers. Raible designed the wheels that were machined by Phil Trenerry.

Tom "Itchy" Otis, from West Hills, California, opened more than a few eyes at the 1993 show with his flamed-and-striped '32 Ford *L.A. Hiboy* roadster. That's Otis waving at me when I snapped this picture! This nostalgic roadster runs with a 327-ci Chevy small-block motor sporting a three-pot Offenhauser manifold topped with Rochester carbs. Rick Cresse filled the grille shell, made the hood, and formed the belly pan. Otis applied the black paint as well as the flames and pinstripes.

Continued from page 98

Among the final inductees in 1966 was Andy Brizio, and when the Hall of Fame was reinstituted in 1988 his son, Roy Brizio, was among the nominees. The junior Brizio

If you went to Oakland in 1993 and voted for entry number 233, you voted for a pedal car. This miniature is one of a kind, built in fiberglass by Jay Bolton of Sacramento. It replicates Norm Grabowski's *Kookie Kar II*. I understand Bolton gave the model to Grabowski after the show. Model cars and miniatures have always been a welcome attraction at Oakland.

was joined by Frank DeRosa (custom car builder), Rod Powell (pinstriper and a painter known for his flamboyant flame graphics), Boyd Coddington (prolific car builder), and Dick Dean (car builder and fabricator, also known as the Dean of Chopped Tops).

Oakland's Hall of Fame was back in business, and every year since 1988 at least two new members have been added to this elite group of car show personalities. Finally,

Kalifornian, built in tribute to George and Sam Barris by Dick Jackson of Paso Robles, California, resembles many of the customs that the Barris brothers built back in the early days of rodding. In fact, as a kid growing up in Lynwood, California, Dick worked for the Barris shop until the most famous name in customizing moved to North Hollywood. Dick's Carson-topped '52 Chevy is his way of saying "thanks" to the Barris Brothers. Additionally, the body has molded lakes pipes, scoops, flush skirts, a '57 Buick grille, frenched headlights, and '60 Corvette taillights. The two-tone candy paint is bisected by a modified '56 Buick side trim.

The first time I saw Tom Prufer's '32 Ford three-window coupe was at the 1993 show. There it sat, bright red, full hood, outside exhausts, and sporting Herb Martinez stripes. The top was filled and chopped four inches, and the car was painted Mazda RX7 Red. The engine is a 427-ci Chevy with two Holley carbs. A Doug Nash T-10 four-speed transmission delivers power to a quick change rear. Sid Chavers did the black Naugahyde interior.

John D'Agostino sits in front of his '57 Caddy El Dorado *Starfire* while a video crew interviews him at the 1993 show. No doubt he's telling them how the car was chopped by Jim Farcello Customs in Nevada, and how other bodywork was done by John Aiellos Jr. & Sr., and Bill Hines. Or he's cluing them in on how Hines painted the gorgeous Candy Red, or how Eddie Martinez of L. A. upholstered the Naugahyde interior with 1 1/4-inch pearl white pleats.

1996's two inductees—famous fabricator and hot rod builder Steve Moal and noted motorcycle customizer Bob Cecchini—put the list at 100. Numbers 101 and 102 were added in 1997 when Ken Fuhrman (whose same Model A roadster that was displayed at the inaugural Oakland Show in 1950 was shown in 1997) and Pete

During my high school days in 1949 I drove a '40 Mercury coupe similar to this! Well, not quite this clean. My old car wasn't chopped or lowered, nor were its flanks as clean thanks, to teardrop fender skirts and molded fenders. But 44 years later, I finally got the '40 Merc of my dreams. I'm proud to say that the car was built by Tom Cutino, of Cutino Customs. My wife, Patty, and I enjoy the car to this very day.

Paulsen (best known as the man who re-invented the custom wheel) were enshrined. The final two members added before the Grand National Roadster Show celebrates its 50th anniversary were custom bike builder Bob Dron and

Rodzy was inspired by a '30s-era tether car built by the Rodzy Company. Mark Morton wanted to have his roadster follow the same style, so he had Pete Eastwood, Steve Davis, and John Carambia lend a hand. A 355 ci-Chevy and Doug Nash five-speed transmission are nestled under the hood, which was modified with '33 side louvers. The windshield is a Hallock, and Steve Davis crafted the top, hood, and louvered side panels. The red leather interior was by Darryl Morgan.

AMBR circa 1994, Joe MacPherson's *Q29 Infinity Flyer*, a '29 Ford body that was re-worked to boast a streamlined look. The customizers responsible for this jewel were: Art & Mike Chrisman, Steve Davis, Hershel "Junior" Conway, Tom Mayfield, and Tony Nancy. The engine is a high-tech 272-ci '92 Infiniti V-8 with a stock five-speed automatic, and a '92 Infiniti third-member adapted to the '32-type frame. Junior applied the Dupont Fly Yellow paint, and Tony Nancy used tan Connally leather for the interior. Looks like Mike Chrisman got stuck with the final cleaning!

pinstriper Herb Martinez, both long-time members of the Bay Area's hot rod clan.

Even though the quality and number of car entries was on the rise, the show's promoters continued an uphill battle with the Oakland Coliseum's management to reserve practical show dates for America's premier hot rod and custom car show. The problem came to a boil in 1997 when the Coliseum complex was under repair to expand the football stadium and to improve the indoor sports arena. Due to the construction schedule, the facility was unable to house the Roadster Show. For the first time since moving into the Coliseum in 1968, the show had to relocate. Rather than move to another venue, Show Promotions, owners of the Roadster Show, remained loyal to the Coliseum, electing to stage the show in temporary quarters in the parking lot. The solution was to erect a pair of huge tents, much like you'd find at a traveling circus. Together the tents offered more than 90,000 square feet of show floor space. Cramped quarters, to be sure, but the die-hard Oakland followers were willing to put up with the inconvenience—for a year, anyway.

It's no surprise that the 1997 show gained several deprecatory nicknames, among them the Big Top Show and Tent City. In any case, the show went on, and Bob Young's 1937 Ford, dubbed *Youngster*, drove off with the AMBR honors. Wrote Bishop about the AMBR winner for *American Rodder* that year, "In years to come, Young's Ford may very well be remembered as 'the one that won in the tent,' "

Regardless of whether Young's AMBR will go down in history as the Tent Winner, the events took an even more sorrowful turn the following year when the Coliseum management scheduled a pair of NCAA college basketball games in the arena on the very dates originally reserved for the 49th Annual Grand National Roadster Show. The Coliseum's management coldly suggested that the car show promoters take their annual event back to the tents. In response, Show Promotions pitched the tent idea, issuing the following press release:

The last picture of the 1994 show is of this beautiful bright red '32 Ford roadster, entered by Chuck and Lois Pixley of Benicia, California. Under the hood sat a 350 Chevy engine dressed with lots of chrome. The side panels were notched with 93 louvers, and the black and white pinstriping has Tommy the Greek overtones thanks to those teardrops on the side cowl.

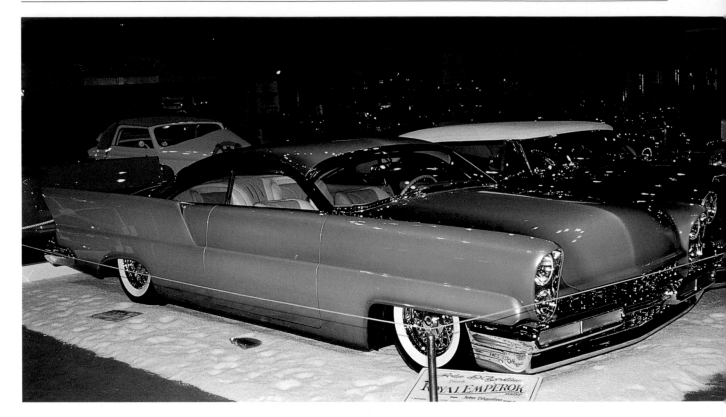

For 1995, John D'Agostino showed his new custom '57 Lincoln Premier hardtop, christened *Royal Emperor*. The bodywork and top were chopped by John Aiello at Sahagon's Custom Car Concepts, Concord, California. The chop top utilized two '57 Lincoln rear windows from a Thom Taylor design. In addition, the body was nosed, decked and dechromed, headlights were frenched and tunneled, and topped with Winfield custom lenses. The body was painted Pearl Mint Green, blended by Winfield, Aiello, and Hollenbeck. The interior is mint green leatherette, English tweed, and Italian jade green velvet, by Sahagon.

Mildred Stevens of Bend, Oregon, showed this unique '32 Chevy roadster pickup at the 1995 show. The pearl white paint and graphics were applied by Art Himsl of Concord. It has four-wheel independent suspension with a quick change center section. Sid Chavers sewed in the white and turquoise Mercedes Benz leather interior.

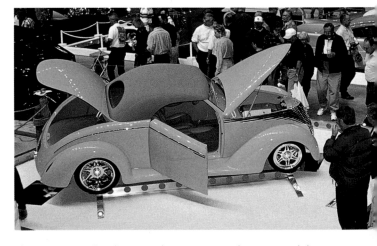

The AMBR award at the 1995 show went to Fred Warren, with his *Smoothster*, a '37 Ford painted pearl yellow. The car was based on a Larry Erickson design, and eventually went to Boyd Coddington, who finished construction for Warren. The car had Corvette front and rear suspension with disc brakes, a '92 Corvette LT1 engine, and 700R4 transmission. The Carson-style one-piece top is covered with dark tan canvas material.

Jose "Pepe" Heredia entered this '55 Mercury Montclair at the 1995 show. A body repairman by trade, Pepe chopped the top three inches, frenched the headlights and taillights, and shaved the door handles and chrome trim. Jose did all the painting, using PPG Blue Metallic, and Rod Powell was called to apply the light blue ghost flames.

"The venerable Grand National Oakland Roadster Show, world's oldest showcase tribute to the American hot rod and custom car art forms, breaks with a near half-century tradition and will hold its 49th edition in San Francisco.

"The event will be held January 16–18 in San Francisco's 140,000 sq. ft. Concourse Exhibition Center at 635 8th St., at the intersection of 8th and Brannan Sts.

"The Roadster Show has been forced to move from its 30-year run at the Oakland Coliseum when Coliseum and Warriors management booked two college basketball games

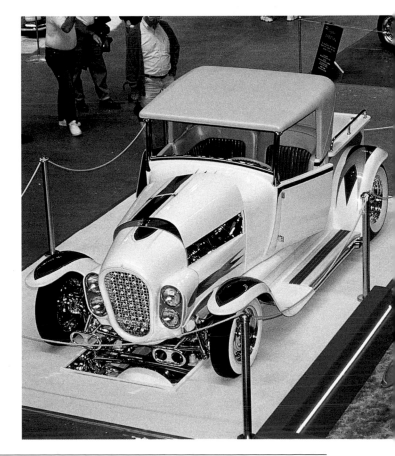

In 1996, Howdy Ledbetter, of Fremont, California, built a custom roadster pickup that resembled Richard Peters' *Ala Kart*. Ledbetter built the car as a tribute, not as a clone, to the first two-time winner of the famed nine-foot trophy. The *Howli Kart*, named after his daughter Howli, featured a chrome Jaguar rear end and a Magnum dropped tube front suspension. The drivetrain was based around a 350 Chevy V-8. Naturally, Ledbetter was responsible for the purple and white Naugahyde upholstery, while fellow Bay Area artisan Art Himsl sprayed on the classic paint job. The *Howli Kart* was finished the morning of the first day of show setup.

In 1996, The Oakland Roadster Show "Builder Of The Year" was Steve Moal, of Oakland, California. Two of his roadsters, a pearl garnet '32 Ford roadster and the *California Special,* were posed alongside each other on the center of the arena floor. The Deuce had a 454 Chevy with a T-10 four-speed transmission, and a polished Halibrand quick change; the *California Special* was a specially built hot rod based on a '50s-era hybrid racer. It was powered by a 239-ci '48 Ford flathead with Offenhauser heads and two carbs. The *Special*'s interior included bucket seats trimmed with Connally red leather.

Oakland Roadster Show Hall Of Fame member Rich Zocchi did an outstanding custom for 1996, entering this '56 Chrysler Windsor. John Aiello chopped the top, taking out 3 3/4 inches. The car was lowered, and all but the side chrome was removed. The grille opening was frenched, and dressed with a cut-down shell and recessed 1-inch bars. Art Himsl sprayed on the aqua pearl and pearl white paint, accenting it with light aqua scallops and violet pinstriping. Jerry Sahagon patterned the Naugahyde and fabric interior to match the car's color.

This '29 Ford A-V8 roadster looks as if it could have appeared at the 1950 Oakland Roadster Show. That's because owner/builder Mike Bishop of Santa Rosa, California, built it that way. He based his roadster on the kind of hot rods that he enjoyed during his high school days. In reality, the steel body is brand new, produced by Brookville Roadsters. Most of the running gear is genuine Ford parts, including a chromed dropped axle, '48 Lincoln brakes, 286-ci '46 Ford flathead, and '39 Ford transmission. The exhaust collectors lead to Smithy's mufflers underneath, and the paint is '36 Ford Washington Blue. And to maintain that old-time theme, the interior was stitched with red Naugahyde.

No, this photo is not flopped. Jeff Black's '32 Ford phaeton started life as an Australian Ford. It became an American hot rod when Jeff channeled the body two inches over the frame, and lowered the roof line eight inches. The engine is a 327-ci '64 Chevy, with a Turbo 350 transmission and Ford rear end. The nostalgic interior was finished with black and white Naugahyde.

The *Mark Of Zocchi*, owned by Richard and Sherry Zocchi of Walnut Creek, California, helped kick off the 1997 show in the tents. This is a beautiful chopped '56 Lincoln Continental Mark II, showing off a custom grille made out of steel rod inside a grille cavity that was formed using pieces from a '51 Merc upper lip. Familiar Zocchi trademarks are the '56 Olds frenched and peaked headlights. In addition, this cool custom had the full body treatment that makes '50s-style customs so popular today. The facelift included a nosed and decked hood, shaved door handles, and pinstriping to contrast the Art Himsl pearl cream-and-yellow paint job. The interior was finished in a subtle cream and yellow cloth/vinyl combination.

The AMBR trophy for 1997 went to Bob Young of Memphis, Tennessee, for his rare 1937 Ford roadster. This was the first—and hopefully only—AMBR to win in a tent! Built by Don Pilkenton of Germantown, Ohio, the roadster has a unique one-piece windshield that was chopped 4 1/2 inches. The leather interior was finished by Lyons Custom Trim & Upholstery, complimenting the Candy Red paint. The remainder of the car's external garments are typical for show hot rods of the '90s, including billet wheels, low-profile radial tires, and a high-tech engine. In this case, power was supplied by a NASCAR-bred 358 Ford V-8, developing 633 horsepower.

right in the middle of the Roadster Show's contracted five-day event dates, January 14–18, 1998.

"'Warriors and Coliseum management suggested we go back to the parking lot and erect tents like we had to do last year when the Arena facility was under construction,' reports Don Tognotti, president of Sacramento's Show Promotions, Inc., and owner of the Grand National Roadster Show.

"'We incurred large losses in the tents last year,' he adds, 'and the prospect of staging another show inside tents during cold, rainy weather was unacceptable.

"'I've decided to let our attorneys handle the Coliseum problem,' he says, 'and secure the Concourse Exhibition Center. This San Francisco site has been selected after an accelerated and exhaustive search for a suitable alternative venue in which to stage this world class, albeit abbreviated, event.'"

Slam dunk, and end of game between the Grand National Roadster Show's promoters and the Oakland

Continued on page 117

Another of the tent cars was this '32 Ford roadster, originally shown at the 1953 National Roadster Show. Since then it has been updated and is owned by Jerry Ash, of Stuart, Florida. The engine remains a Ford flathead, and it's equipped with rare Ardun heads and a 4-71 BDS blower. Notice the chrome outside headers have bypasses to mufflers underneath. The pearl orange-cream paint was done by Rick Carrol. The Connally leather upholstery is by Jeffrey Phipps. Those classy chrome wire wheels are from a '53 Buick Skylark.

Oakland entries hail from all over the country. In 1998 Jack Merrill entered his '32 from Pueblo, Colorado. This beautiful blue, yellow, orange, silver, and magenta '32 roadster was built by Zipper, basing the project on a Jerry Kugel Speedster body and frame. The frame rails were pinched two inches and lengthened six inches to accommodate the all-Chevy drivetrain and Kugel Komponents IRS system. The roadster is a driver, too.

Right
Dave and Joyce Emery of Rochester Hills, Michigan, showed up at San Francisco with their '32 Ford roadster, nicknamed *Revolver*. This straight-shooter scored a bull's-eye the year before, winning the coveted Don Ridler Award at the '97 Detroit Autorama. Next, the Emerys set their sights on Oakland/San Francisco to win the 1998 AMBR award where, once again, it was right on target. The '32 Ford is based on a Zipper fiberglass body painted Candy Red and black by Guy Wolcott.

Next Page
Bruce Meyer of Beverly Hills, California, never ceases to amaze me. He's meticulous with all of his restored hot rods. Here is one that he recently resurrected, truly capturing 1950s vintage style. *Ruby Red* has a '50 Mercury V-8 with Ardun overhead conversion for power, a traditional black Naugahyde interior, and wide whitewall tires. This nostalgic rod resembled hot rods of the '50s, right down to the NHRA decal on the windshield.

Customs were quite prevalent at the 1998 show. One outstanding '51 Chevy fastback, nicknamed *Gold Dust*, belonged to Leo Reyes of San Jose, California. Tom Cutino, of Cutino's Custom Shop, chopped the top 3 1/2 inches, frenched the headlights, rounded the hood corners, and inserted a custom grille. Carlos Lima's Elegance Auto Body applied the pearl yellow paint, and Soft Top finished the project with pearl white upholstery.

The 1998 show had another nostalgic hot rod, a '28 Ford roadster pickup entered by Dan and Marguerita Capp of Napa, California. The A-pickup's parts manifesto reads like an old-time hot rod parts list: dropped and chromed front axle, filled '32 Ford grille shell, black paint with red and white striping, and chromed steelie wheels. And in the tradition of Oakland show cars, the engine and its three carbs were dressed with chromed and polished goodies, and the interior boasts neatly pleated red Naugahyde.

Continued from page 110

Coliseum management. The 50th anniversary show for 1999 also was rescheduled, to be held at the Cow Palace in South San Francisco, to coincide with the show's traditional show dates over President's Weekend (February 10–15, 1999).

Ironically, back in 1951, Al Slonaker had begun to lay plans to hold the second annual show in San Francisco, but that never evolved, leading to an Oakland tradition that lasted until 1998. Regardless of where the show was—or is—held, the fact remains that everybody involved—car owners and spectators alike—don't care *where* it is held so much as that it *is* held. Wrote Geisert for *Street Rodder* about the 1998 show, "The fact [that] it was held in San Francisco this year didn't change what this indoor event is all about: gathering the best of the best for a car show in the grandest tradition."

Most important of all, despite friction from the Oakland Coliseum management, the show went on. In the process, Show Promotions and everybody involved proved to themselves and the show world that the Grand National Roadster Show is a success due to the show itself, rather than its location. Wrote Bishop in an editorial for *American Rodder*, "The show itself is wonderful and winds up with no more than the usual ration of gripes about who won what and who didn't; Oakland or not, it's still a car show. Slam-dunk."

Given the amount of press the Grand National Roadster Show received during the past decade that also coincides with the end of the millennium, it's fitting that we close with a final quote from a member of the automotive world's fourth estate. In a report about Oakland a few years ago that Jerry Weesner penned for *Street Rodder* magazine, he wrote:

"Oakland is an annual gathering place for the great and not so great of car and bike building. It's for luminaries of the hobby, and those who just like to hang with the crowd of like-minded folks. At Oakland you can meet and talk with people who you've only read about (all the way back to the little 25-cent magazines). They're real, they're approachable. They're car guys, and they're happy to be there . . . THEY'RE AT OAKLAND!"

By 1998 the Oakland Roadster Show had become home for some really tasty customs, too. Rick and Susan Dore of Glendale, Arizona, entered this out-a-site convertible. Inspired by Steve Stanford's rendition of a '36 that appeared in *Street Rodder* magazine., the Ford was customized just in the nick of time for the 1998 Oakland show. Beneath the beautiful pearl tangerine paint includes new-wave custom hardware such as air-bag suspension and a Chevy 350 engine. Topside you can see the obvious, such as the chopped top, '40 Packard grille, '37 Buick headlights, molded running boards, and custom '39 Lincoln Zephyr fenders and skirts.

FEATURES INCLU
· MONROE COIL SPRINGS/SHOC
· STEWART-WARNER INSTRUMEN
· HAYDEN TRANS COOLER
· EELCO FUEL SYSTEM
· CRAGAR STEERING WHEEL
INTERIOR | BODY DEVELOPMENT | GAS TA
TONY NANCY | GEORGE BARRIS | CAL AUTO

![Trophy with number 6]

America's Most Beautiful Roadster
Taking Home The Gold

So what's it like to win the nine-foot-tall trophy that stands majestically for all the goodness ever created in a hot rod roadster? Andy Brizio, the winner of America's Most Beautiful Roadster award in 1970, explains it in a single sentence, "It was probably the biggest thrill in my life at the time."

Indeed, you'll probably hear hyperbole such as that from most of the AMBR winners, for many car builders put blood, sweat, and tears—and a lot of money these days—into the cars. No doubt, all winners take the contest seriously, or they probably wouldn't have built the car in the first place. But in some instances, owners and builders become so engrossed in winning the trophy that they place the award on a high pedestal. Eventually they become so consumed by the thought of owning the most beautiful roadster in the country that they lose sight of why they enjoy hot rods in the first place, and that's to experience the

For the year 1963, LeRoy "Tex" Smith was the AMBR winner with his specially built roadster, *XR-6*. The roadster was designed by Steve Swaja, and built by Barris, Winfield, Gordon Vann and Tex as a project car for *Hot Rod* magazine. The project started life as a '27 Model T body on a tube chassis with a Volkswagen front end. Rear suspension was from a Dodge Dart. The engine—an aluminum slant-six— was also pirated from the Dart. It was mated to a Torqueflite transmission. The paint was typical Barris—Candy Tangerine Metalflake. The beige Naugahyde upholstery was by Tony Nancy.

Trivial Pursuit
Some Interesting Facts About Past AMBR Winners

- The AMBR trophy was originally advertised to be eight feet tall.
- Only roadsters manufactured before 1938, or hand-built roadsters, are eligible for the award.
- The first AMBR winner was Bill NeiKamp's 1929 Ford.
- The first co-winners were Blackie Gejeian and Ray Anderegg in 1955. Ironically, both had 1927 Fords. Additional co-winners include Bob Reisner's *Invader* and Joe Wilhelm's *Wild Dream* in 1968. Both of these winners were based on custom-made bodies.
- The first two-time winner was Richard Peters' *Ala Kart*, 1958 and 1959.
- All but 11 winning entries have been from California.
- Six winners have been from Fresno, California, the most of any city.
- All winning cars have been Fords or custom-built roadsters.
- The earliest-year car to win has been Don Tognotti's 1914 Model T roadster (1964) and Jim Vasser's 1914 Model T touring (1974).
- The latest-year car to win has been Fred Warren's 1937 Ford (1995), and Bob Young's 1937 Ford (1997).
- From 1957 through 1971 the 9-foot trophy was shared by America's Most Beautiful Roadster and America's Best Competition Car (five of these winners were from Oakland).
- The person to win the AMBR the most times is Ermie Immerso (1988, 1989, 1991).

thrill of building a car like no other on the road.

No doubt, through the years, competition for the nine-footer has been fierce. Blackie Gejeian, winner in 1955, says that too often AMBR candidates become consumed by their chase to win the award. "Some people spend too much on their cars," says Blackie. "If they lose, they get disappointed. I saw one guy just up and quit because he had nearly $200,000 in his car, and he lost. So he sold it all, and that was that."

Adds Don Tognotti, winner of the Big One in 1964 and current promoter of the Oakland show, "Rejection is hard, no matter what part of life you're talking about." In short, you win some, you lose some, or as he puts it, "Not everyone who comes to our shows wins a trophy."

The attitudes were different during the early years, recalls Blackie. "There's a lot of difference in showing cars in those days," he points out. "It was a real sport back then. We used to shake the winner's hand. Nobody got real upset, or said it was politics or anything."

Fact is, the early-day AMBR winners were perhaps a little too lax in their attitude for the award. Don't be misled, they were grateful to win the prestigious award, but when it came time to accept the gargantuan trophy, they lost a little of their enthusiasm and responsibility, because the winner got to—no, make that *had to*—take the trophy home, and baby-sit it for the subsequent 12 months until he could pass it off to the next winner. As you can imagine, trailering a loving cup that's taller than any basketball star who's ever played in the Oakland Arena proved to be a lesson in logistics, and often the trip home was met with complications. There are even unsubstantiated rumors that at least one AMBR winner dropped the trophy from the back of his pickup truck while transporting the loving cup home.

No doubt, the years of mistreatment took its toll on the trophy, and it has been repaired at least twice. Brizio rebuilt it once, and the most recent rehab was conducted by current Oakland promoter Tognotti, who kiddingly says, "I'm still packing this trophy!"

As you can imagine, the big cup has been considered an albatross around the winner's neck, for nobody *really* wanted to haul around a 100-pound chunk of wood and brass for 12 months. Says Tognotti, "You don't realize how tall it is until you get the damn thing."

So, how did the winners truly feel about the trophy that became known as The Big One, or the "granddaddy goody, the nine-footer," as Tex Smith once described the trophy? Well, let's let good ol' boy Tex himself tell you. The following excerpt is from a story Tex wrote in *Rod & Custom* when he reminisced about the time he won the granddaddy goody in 1963. The exposé centers around a conversation he had with co-winner Bob Tindle. (For the years 1957 through 1971, the trophy was shared by the AMBR recipient and the winner of America's Best Competition Car, each strapping the albatross trophy around their necks for six months apiece.) Here is Tex's account, as it appeared in the May 1967 issue of *Rod & Custom*:

"Like I said way back when, someday I was gonna win that award, and I finally did with the *XR-6* roadster. There I was, in that great gaping barn of a building, fending off dive-bombing birds, polishing the car (which I dearly hate to do), when Bob Tindle (he owns the *Orange Crate*, a beautiful '32 competition sedan) dropped by. 'So whatcha gonna do with the big cup, Texas, 'cause you're sure to win it this year?'"

Continued Tex in his show report for *R&C*: "'Oh, I won't get it Bob. It would be nice, but, naw, that'll never happen.' I secretly wanted it to happen very, very much, but then a horrible thought crossed the brain. What in the world would I do with a nine-foot trophy weighing over 100 pounds? Oh, good gosh; rangle tangle ratchet wrench!

"Sure enough, it happened. 'OK, ol' Tex buddy, tell you what,' beamed Tindle, after he had been announced the co-winner, a repeat for him. 'You take the big cup home for six months, then I'll take it for six.'

"'Uh, no Bob, I don't have my truck here, and I can't get it home. Besides, since it's a second time for you, wouldn't those Portland folks like to see it again?'

"'Nope.'

"'Well, gee whiz guy . . .' And there standing in the exit door is glowering assistant show manager Mel Fernandez. Mel is also the assistant starter for the Indianapolis 500 race, and when he glowers at you, you been glowered."

At this point in Tex's tale, the dialogue gets testy, as Fernandez did what he did best in those days, and that was to take charge of the situation. Tex continued, repeating Fernandez's brief, yet crystal-clear command:

"'Go!'" (To use an oft-used Tex Smith phrase, 'Nuff said. And so Tex took the trophy home, as he further related in his story.)

With a single word Tex cooled the heels of a glowering Fernandez. "'Yezzir.'

"So whattaya do with a trophy taller than your living room?" wrote Tex. "You lay it down behind the couch ('Oh, yes, we like it cozy that way') and try to be casual about the whole thing ('Oh, it's just a little old thing my husband picked up at a car show.').

"Which reminds me Bob Tindle, you never did serve your six months," concluded Tex. End of dialogue, and end of Tex's story.

But not the end of the Big One, and to this day the trophy thrives, although now the winner is given a small replica, while the original "Granddaddy Goody" remains safe and sound at Show Promotions' headquarters in Sacramento where it awaits the next Grand National Roadster Show.

The biggest thrill in car show history lives on. And so does the biggest trophy that you can win with a hot rod roadster.

Appendix

America's Most Beautiful Roadster

Year	Owner	Car	Year	Owner	Car
1950	Bill NeiKamp	1929 Ford roadster	1974	Jim Vasser	1914 Ford touring
1951	Rico Squaglia	1923 Ford roadster	1975	Lonnie Gilbertson	1923 Ford roadster pickup
1952	Bud Crackbon	1925 Ford roadster	1976	Bob Sbarbaro	1923 Ford touring
1953	Dick Williams	1927 Ford roadster	1977	Jim Molino	1923 Ford roadster pickup (*Candy Man*)
1954	Frank Rose	1927 Ford roadster			
1955	Blackie Gejeian	1927 Ford roadster (*Chicken Coop*)	1978	Phil Cool	1932 Ford roadster
1955	Ray Anderegg	1927 Ford roadster	1979	Brian Burnett	1932 Ford roadster (*Deucari*)
1956	Eddie Bosio	1932 Ford roadster	1980	John Corno	1929 Ford roadster
1957	Jerry Woodward	1929 Ford roadster	1981	John Siroonian	1932 Ford roadster
1958	Richard Peters	1929 Ford roadster pickup (*Ala Kart*)	1982	Jamie Musselman	1933 Ford roadster
1959	Richard Peters	1929 Ford roadster pickup (*Ala Kart*)	1983	Chuck Lombardo	1932 Ford roadster
1960	Chuck Krikorian	1929 Ford roadster (*Emperor*)	1984	Don Varner	1927 Ford roadster (*California Star*)
1961	Rich Guasco	1929 Ford roadster	1985	Larry & Judi Murray	1933 Ford phaeton
1962	George Barris	1927 Ford roadster (*Twister T*)	1986	Jim McNamara	1933 Ford roadster
1963	LeRoi "Tex" Smith	1927 Ford roadster (*XR-6*)	1987	James Ells	1932 Ford roadster
1964	Don Tognotti	1914 Ford roadster (*King T*)	1988	Ermie Immerso	1932 Ford roadster (*Orange Crush*)
1965	Carl Casper	custom body (*Casper's Ghost*)	1989	Ermie Immerso	1925 Ford roadster (*Golden Star*)
1966	Don Lokey	1927 Ford roadster pickup	1990	Butch Martino	1932 Ford roadster (*Passion*)
1967	Bob Reisner	custom body (*Invader*)	1991	Ermie Immerso	1925 Ford roadster (*Golden Star*)
1968	Bob Reisner	custom body (*Invader*)	1992	Dennis Varni	1929 Ford roadster
1968	Joe Wilhelm	custom body (*Wild Dream*)	1993	Don Raible	1932 Ford roadster (*Blu Steel*)
1969	Art & Mickey Himsl	custom body (*Alien*)	1994	Joe MacPherson	1929 Ford roadster (*Infinity Flyer*)
1970	Andy Brizio	1923 Ford roadster pickup (*Instant T*)	1995	Fred Warren	1937 Ford roadster (*Smoothster*)
1971	Lonnie Gilbertson	1923 Ford roadster pickup	1996	Boyd Coddington	1932 Ford roadster (*Boydster*)
1972	John Corno	1930 Ford roadster	1997	Bob Young	1937 Ford roadster (*Youngster*)
1973	Chuck Corsello	1923 Ford roadster	1998	Dave Emery	1932 Ford roadster

America's Best Competition Car—1957–1971

Year	Owner	Car
1957	Ed & Ray Cortopassi	Dragster *Glass Slipper*
1958	Romeo Palamides	Dragster
1959	Henry Vincent	Dragster *Top Banana*
1960	Gary McArthur	Dragster
1961	Bob Tindle	1932 Ford sedan *Orange Crate*
1962	Richard Guasco	Fiat roadster *Pure Hell*
1963	Bob Tindle	1932 Ford sedan *Orange Crate*
1964	Dorricott & Sheehan	Fiat coupe
1965	Nick Mura	1940 Willys
1966		
1967		
1968		
1969	Jim Gonsalves	Dragster
1970	Mike Mitchell	1969 Corvette Funny Car
1971	Tony Del Rio	1927 Ford Roadster

Hall Of Fame Inductee List

1960

Al Slonaker
Joe Bailon
George Barris
Mrs. Harold Casaurang
Ezra Ehrhardt
Romeo Palamides
Wally Parks
Robert E. Petersen
Gordon Vann
Walto Woron

1961

Chic Cannon
Dick Day
Fred Esser
Blackie Gejeian
Hoard Leever
Richard Peters
Guy Root
Gene Winfield

1962

Bob Accosta
Harold "Baggy" Bagdasarian
Jack Hagemann Sr.
Dean Moon
Eric Rickman
Jerry Sahagon
Mary Slonaker
Joe Wilhelm
Lee Wood
Jerry Woodward

1963

Donald Bell
Bill Cushenbery
Ted Frye
Frank Livingston
Bob McNulty
Ak Miller
Barbara Parks
LeRoi "Tex" Smith
Darryl Starbird

1964

Paul Bender
E. J. "Bud" Coons

1965

Tony Del Rio
Mike Homen
Beverley Johnson
Kenny Leevenberg
Wilbert "Sonny" Morris
William Penland
Don Tognotti
Fred Agabashian
Harry Costa

1966

Andy Brizio
Ray Brock
Carl Casper
Jim Giminez
Don Lokey
Chuck Trantham
Joe Cruces
Bob Larivee
Dave Puhl

Hall of Fame suspended activity from 1967 until 1988

1988

Roy Brizio
Frank DeRosa
Rod Powell
Boyd Coddington
Dick Dean

1989

Tom Medley
Bud Millard
Arlen Ness

1990

Ken Foster
Tom Prufer
Norm Grabowski

1991

Richard Zocchi
Jack Hagemann Jr.
Andy Southard Jr.

1992

Ray Smith
Hank Medeiros
Bill Reasoner
Art Himsl
Kent Fuller

1993

Mike Alexander
Larry Alexander
Von Dutch
Rick Perry
Bill Hines
Greg Sharp
Gray Baskerville

1994

Gil Ayala
Bill Burnham
Hershel Conway
Howdy Ledbetter

1995

Sam Barris
John D'Agostino
Sam Foose
Rich Pichette

1996

Steve Moal
Bob Checchini

1997

Pete Paulsen
Ken Fuhrman

1998

Bob Dron
Herb Martinez

Al Slonaker Memorial Award

Year	Owner/Person	Vehicle
1974	Bob Reed	
1975	John Buttera	1926 Ford
1976	Jack Walker	Corvette
1977	Syd DeSota	1956 Harley-Davidson
1978	Dusty Santos	1977 Jeep
1979	Ken Nannerhorn	1926 Ford
1980	Ed Papac	1964 Volkswagen
1981	Vern Luce	1933 Ford
1982	Jay Ohrberg	1932 Ford
1983	Bob Checchin	1957 Chevrolet
1984	Ed Gonsalves	1971 Corvette
1985	Steve Lykens	1932 Ford
1986	James Winfrey	1966 Corvette
1987	Frank DeRosa	1951 Mercury
1988	Chris Addington	Karmann-Ghia Volkswagen
1989	Jim Thayer	
1990	Bernt Karlsson	1955 Volkswagen
1991	Bill Abate	1956 Lincoln
1992	Bob Dron	1992 Harley-Davidson
1993	David Sellers	1984 Jeep CJ7
1994	Dan Fink	1932 Ford
1995	Richard Mattioli	1940 Ford
1996	Leonard Lopez	1940 Ford
1997	Fred Warren	1937 Ford
1998	Tom Armstrong	1954 Corvette Nomad

Builder Of The Year

Year	Builder	Type of Vehicle
1987	Joe Bailon	Custom Cars
1988	Boyd Coddington	Hot Rods
1989	Gene Winfield	Custom Cars
1990	Roy Brizio	Hot Rods
1991	Frank DeRosa	Custom Cars
1992	Howdy Ledbetter	Hot Rods
1993	Bill Reasoner	Custom Cars
1994	Arlen Ness	Motorcycles
1995	Art Himsl	Custom Cars and Hot Rods
1996	Steve Moal	Custom Cars and Hot Rods
1997	Sam Foose	Custom Cars and Hot Rods
1998	Bill Hines	Custom Cars
1999	George Barris	Custom Cars and Hot Rods
2000	Ron Simms	Motorcycles

George Barris Kustom d'Elegance Award

Year	Car	Owner
1992	Richard Zocchi	1939 Dodge
1993	Jack Walker & Tim Savage	1941 Ford
1994	Frank Livingston & Richard Zocchi	1951 Oldsmobile
1995	Mike Young & Jimmy Vaughn	1960 Chevrolet
1996	David Fagundes	1949 Mercury
1997	Joe & Carol Cusumano	1957 Chevrolet
1998	Helga Noteboom	1949 Cadillac

Von Dutch Award

Year	Car	Owner
1994	Tom Skinner/Herb Martinez	1950 Mercury
1995		
1996	Dean Murry/Bob Hovack	1929 Ford
1997	Gary Schroeder/Rick Creese	1927 Ford
1998	Bob & Jody Eichensehr/Mike Farley	1931 Ford

Brizio Family Award

Year	Car	Owner
1995	Steve Moal	1932 Ford
1996	Sam Foose	1941 Ford
1997	Don & Marscha Cameron	1932 Ford
1998	Dave & Carol Schaub	1934 Ford

Bruce Meyer Hot Rod Preservation Perpetual Trophy

Year	Car	Owner
1997	Bary Schroeder & Rick Creese	1927 Ford
1998	Tommy Clawson	1932 Ford

Crescent Truck Lines Award

Year	Car	Owner
1998	Arland Cook	1947 Ford

Steve Archer Award

Year	Car	Owner
1998	Paul Weggerman	1927 Ford

Index